D0945346

the pathway
to success

the pathway to success

success

LETTING GOD LEAD YOU TO A LIFE OF MEANING AND PURPOSE

JOYCE MEYER

New York • Nashville

Copyright © 2024 by Joyce Meyer

Cover design by Whitney J. Hicks.
Cover copyright © 2024 by Hachette Book Group, Inc.

Hachette Book Group supports the right to free expression and the value of copyright. The purpose of copyright is to encourage writers and artists to produce the creative works that enrich our culture.

The scanning, uploading, and distribution of this book without permission is a theft of the author's intellectual property. If you would like permission to use material from the book (other than for review purposes), please contact permissions@hbgusa.com. Thank you for your support of the author's rights.

FaithWords
Hachette Book Group
1290 Avenue of the Americas, New York, NY 10104
faithwords.com
twitter.com/faithwords

First Edition: February 2024

FaithWords is a division of Hachette Book Group, Inc. The FaithWords name and logo are trademarks of Hachette Book Group, Inc.

The publisher is not responsible for websites (or their content) that are not owned by the publisher.

The Hachette Speakers Bureau provides a wide range of authors for speaking events. To find out more, go to hachettespeakersbureau.com or email HachetteSpeakers@hbgusa.com.

FaithWords books may be purchased in bulk for business, educational, or promotional use. For information, please contact your local bookseller or the Hachette Book Group Special Markets Department at special.markets@hbgusa.com.

Library of Congress Cataloging-in-Publication Data
Names: Meyer, Joyce, author.
Title: The pathway to success : letting God lead you to a life of meaning and purpose / Joyce Meyer.
Description: First edition. | New York, NY : FaithWords, 2024.
Identifiers: LCCN 2023036587 | ISBN 9781546029229 (hardcover) | ISBN 9781546004882 | ISBN 9781546029205 (ebook)
Subjects: LCSH: Success—Religious aspects—Christianity.
Classification: LCC BV4598.3 .M474 2024 | DDC 158—dc23/eng/20230928
LC record available at https://lccn.loc.gov/2023036587

ISBNs: 978-1-5460-2922-9 (hardcover), 978-1-5460-0488-2 (large type), 978-1-5460-2920-5 (ebook)

Printed in the United States of America

LSC-H

Printing 1, 2023

Contents

Introduction

Most people want to succeed. God also wants us to succeed. But it is important to understand that what God considers success is not always what the world considers success.

The world considers people successful when they have a lot of money, own their own business, hold executive positions, or achieve fame and recognition. People with well-respected careers, such as doctors and lawyers, are viewed as successful, as are actors, actresses, singers, and celebrity athletes. Highly educated people and those regarded as experts in their field are also thought of as successful. But as Christians, we don't base success on the same criteria the world uses. The Bible teaches that we are *in* the world but not *of* the world, and that we are not to be worldly (John 17:11, 14–15; Romans 12:2).

The backgrounds and behind-the-scenes lives of many people the world considers successful reveal that they are unhappy, unkind, unloving, or self-absorbed. We also hear that they sometimes struggle with substance abuse and relational problems. They may work hard to obtain the positions they have, only to discover that they are unfulfilled and really don't know who they are apart from what they do.

Recently someone told me he had been in a respected profession for twenty-five years. He is now retired and said he felt he had lost his identity. He said, "I used to be at the top of my profession, and now I am nothing." A child of God never has to feel this way because we know we are much more than what we do. We find our value in our relationship with God through Christ. God loves us, and having His love is more important than having anything else. Isn't it good to know that God doesn't love us for what we do, but He loves us because we are His children?

We find our value in our relationship with God through Christ.

In addition to what I have already mentioned, many so-called successful people are lonely. They have put all their time and energy into being at the top of their profession and as a result, they often do not have meaningful relationships.

For many people, their primary pursuit in life is making money. If this is your top priority, you will be sadly disappointed when you discover that money cannot keep you happy. Are you working two jobs to pay for a house you wanted, while ignoring your relationships with God and your family? Are you so busy working to pay for your house that you have no time to enjoy living in it? Many years from now, that house may not be fit for anyone to live in. Or maybe it's a car you are working for; someday it will just be a piece of metal in a junkyard.

The Bible also reveals that everything in this world is currently passing away. In the end, only God will remain, so He should be our top priority above all else.

First John 2:15–17 says:

Do not love the world or anything in the world. If anyone loves the world, love for the Father is not in them. For everything in the world—the lust of the flesh, the lust of the eyes, and the pride of life—comes not from the Father but from the world. The world and its desires pass away, but whoever does the will of God lives forever.

Jesus tells us in Matthew 6:19, "Do not store up for yourselves treasures on earth, where moths and vermin destroy, and where thieves break in and steal."

Revelation 18:10–11 says that Babylon (which I believe represents the world system) will fall in one hour and that the "merchants of the earth" (representing those who deal in commerce) will mourn. I was not alive during the Great Depression in 1929, but in one day, people who had a great deal of money in the morning had nothing by the end of the day. The stock market crashed, jobs were scarce, and money that people had worked years to save vanished in just a few hours. Having money is fine, but we should never put our hope in it, because it is not stable. However, God is faithful, and He never changes (Hebrews 13:8).

In this book, I hope to help you understand how

to walk the pathway to success in your life. The success we want is what God considers success, not success as the world views it. In God's kingdom, people may be world-famous or wealthy; they may own businesses, be CEOs of major corporations, be movie stars or sports celebrities, or appear successful for other reasons. But their motivation will be to do these things for God's glory, not merely to feel important and make money. They will also desire to share what they have with people in need.

The success we want is what God considers success, not success as the world views it.

God wants you to succeed in everything He calls and equips you to do, and my prayer is that this book will guide you down the pathway to true godly success.

1

&

What Is in Your Heart?

&

Success is not the key to happiness. Happiness is the key to success. If you love what you are doing, you will be successful.

Albert Schweitzer[1]

On the pathway to success, the first questions I want to ask you are: What is in your heart? What do you want to do with your life? If you aren't sure, you may have to try some things and see if they fit you. Here's an example to explain what I mean. If I shop for an outfit for a special occasion, I may try on five or six options before I find the one that fits just right and feels comfortable to me. This is a good way to think about how to find your pathway in life. What fits? What is comfortable? What do you like to do? What are you good at?

God gives us desires, and He frequently speaks to us through them. God won't call you to do something you hate, just as I would not buy an outfit that was uncomfortable and didn't look good on me.

God will give you a desire to do something that fits you and that you enjoy. I've discovered that you know you are on the pathway to success if you would do your job without being paid for it.

You are on the pathway to success if you would do your job without being paid for it.

WHAT WAS IN MY HEART

I will share more about my personal pathway to success in the next chapter of this book, but here I simply want to say that I know what it's like to have a dream in your heart and wonder how it will ever come to pass. I know what it's like to have a desire that means everything to me, a desire that only God can fulfill. And thankfully, by God's grace, I know how it feels to pray, work, and believe that He will make a dream come true in His perfect timing. I have walked the journey to success God's way and learned many lessons along the way—lessons I hope and pray will help and encourage you as you continue through this book.

After I began seriously walking with God and felt called to teach His Word, I started a small Bible study in my home. During the years I taught this home Bible study, I was happy, but I wanted to do more. However, I had to go through a testing time before more came. During that season, I tried a lot of different things because I was zealous for God. I gathered a group of ladies, and in one summer, we distributed ten thousand gospel tracts, putting them under car windshield wipers. I tried working in the church nursery but dreaded it every time I went, so I only did it for two or three weeks. I cleaned my pastor's home a couple of times. I tried doing street witnessing or evangelism on weekends, and I was so uncomfortable I dreaded every Saturday morning. At one point, I even tried to be my pastor's secretary, but at the end of the first day, he told me he didn't think that was where I belonged. I had to try all these things before I finally realized that teaching the Bible is the best fit for me. But I wanted to do a lot more than teach a small Bible study in my home. I was consumed with a passion to teach God's Word all over the world.

Your desire may not be to be on a platform or stage, to head a corporation, own your own business, or be world-famous. It may be to raise amazing children, be the best wife in the world, or to write a cookbook. It could be to own a bakery. It doesn't matter what your dream is, as long as it's what you really want to do and believe with all your heart that God wants you to do it. Success is doing whatever we do for God and doing it in a way that pleases and brings glory to Him.

Success is doing whatever we do for God in a way that pleases and brings glory to Him.

If everyone were a preacher or a worship leader, the world wouldn't work right. There are thousands of jobs that need to be filled. Dave and I marvel at the people who wash windows on high-rise buildings or work with the public and listen to people complain. I frequently say, "Thank God, I'm not a waitress," but some people love waiting tables and have done it for many years. Dave says, "I thank God you are not a cook." I did cook three meals a day for many years while we were raising our children, but those days are long gone. The last time I tried to fry an egg for Dave, I cracked it, totally missed the skillet, and dropped it into the stove burner. I have definitely moved on to other things!

FOLLOW YOUR HEART, NOT
YOUR EMOTIONS

Some people have what others might consider "ordinary" lives that aren't exciting or fulfilling, but for those people, life is not ordinary in a negative way as long as it fits them and makes them happy. It's so important that each of us chooses to do what God puts in our heart to do. Don't let other people push you into doing things that make you miserable, no matter how much they think you should do them.

Psalm 1:1 says we are not to take counsel from the ungodly. Certainly, this means not to take the advice of ungodly people, but it could also mean not allowing ourselves to be led by our emotions or thoughts that don't agree with God's Word. If the dreams in my heart require sacrifice, I may not *feel* like doing it, and my mind may find many reasons not to do it. But I need to look past all that and see what God has put in my heart, because ultimately that is the only thing that will satisfy me. In addition, I need to believe I am pleasing God with my decision. Because trying to do something with a guilty heart won't make you happy. You must be confident that what you are doing is right in God's eyes; otherwise, there is no point in doing it.

Multitudes of people ask, "What does God want me to do?" or "How can I know what God wants me to do?" First, it should agree with God's Word. It should be something you have a desire to do, will enjoy doing, and believe God has anointed you—or given you the ability— to do. God's anointing is His presence and power. When you do the thing He's given you a desire to do, you sense that God's presence and His power are with you. This does not mean you never have to do anything you don't really want to do or don't feel like doing. We are all called to make sacrifices at times, but I am referring to your life's calling. Where that's concerned, you should have a desire to do it. I don't believe God calls people to do things as their life's work that they would not enjoy or that would make them unhappy for the rest of their lives.

AVOID ASKING YOURSELF THE WRONG QUESTIONS

When you have a strong desire to do something, don't ask yourself how you *feel* about doing certain necessary aspects of it. I remember when someone asked me, "How do you feel about all the travel you have to do in order to succeed at what God has asked you to do?"

I thought for a moment and said, "I haven't asked myself that question in a long, long time." It doesn't matter how I feel about traveling. The questions that matter are, am I fulfilled in doing it, and do I believe I am doing what God wants me to do? And the answer is yes. I may not enjoy certain parts of my job, such as traveling, packing and unpacking, and staying in various hotels. But I love, love, love my overall job! The truth is that there is no job in which we will enjoy every little thing that's required. We have to look at everything involved as a whole, and when we are doing what God has for us to do, we will find that we love more about it than we dislike.

Don't waste time asking yourself what you think about this or that, because our thoughts and feelings can change from one hour to the next. For example, I can think I want to do something, and an hour later I think I don't want to do it. Our thoughts are changeable and unreliable when they are simply based on what we feel. One thought can tell you to do something because it will be fun, and the next one can tell you the same activity will be too hard. Don't ask yourself what you think. Instead, focus your mind on God for a while, pray and ask Him to show you what is in your heart. This will help you find the right thing to do.

I remember a woman who had no strong desire to do anything in particular. She was greatly frustrated because of this for a long time. Then God led her to Psalm 100:2, which says, "Serve the Lord with gladness!" (AMPC), and she decided that serving Him gladly was the call on her life. Some people are encouragers, some are helpers, some are organizers, and some do a host of other things that don't fit into the world's standard of success. So don't think you are doing something unimportant just because the world would not consider it great. Some of the most important people in my life are those who help me with the practical details of my life and the ones who pray for me and encourage me. The bottom line is that whatever God gives you to do is important, no matter what it is.

FAILURE IS PART OF SUCCESS

I like this quotation, which is often attributed to Winston Churchill: "Failure is not fatal. It is the courage to continue that counts."

I am convinced that if you will never give up, you will eventually end up at the perfect place for you. I have often said that I believe my greatest gift is the refusal to give up. I will not quit! The Bible is filled with scriptures encouraging us not to give up. People often ask me if I am going to retire, and I tell them I haven't given retirement much thought. If I begin to think about it too much, I may grow weak and feel I can't go on for some reason. Most of the time I feel young on the inside, so I am going to act young on the outside.

I believe my greatest gift is the refusal to give up.

I understand that I will have to adjust my schedule as the years go by, and I will use wisdom. But I don't plan to get to the point where I just sit in a chair and do nothing day after day. I don't know when or if I will retire from teaching God's Word like I've been doing for more than forty years now. I have no plans to do so, but I will do whatever God guides me to do.

On our way to success, we will fail sometimes and have to adjust our plans. John Maxwell wrote a book called *Failing Forward*, and I think the idea of failing forward is great. This basically means that we let our failures become stepping-stones to the future instead of allowing them to hold us back. We are wise when we learn from our mistakes rather than feel guilty about them.

I have made many mistakes, but I have also experienced many successes. If you let every failure devastate you, you will not succeed at what you really want to do. God knows your heart, and as long as you sincerely want to do His will, even if you veer onto the wrong pathway, He will gently guide you back onto the right one.

You will not succeed if you let failure devastate you.

For example, I tried to go on television long before the time was right. We rented a local cable studio, and I tried to do a talk show. I sat down with three or four people who worked for me, and I asked them questions. But the problem was that I also answered the questions. You can't have a talk show if you are the only one who talks. Over the course of six months, we only received one piece of mail in response to the program, and I realized I was on the wrong path. After that, I forgot all about television and was surprised when God later showed us that He wanted us to produce a television show. I realized that it was part of God's plan all along, but I wasn't following His time frame the first time around. Sometimes we know in our hearts what God's will is, but we get ahead of His timing.

Sometimes we let ourselves get ahead of God's timing.

Let me say again that feeling guilty about your mistakes is useless. We all make mistakes. When you make one, simply ask God to forgive you and show you how to begin again.

The apostle Paul writes:

I do not consider, brethren, that I have captured and made it my own [yet]; but one thing I do [it is my one aspiration]: forgetting what lies behind and straining forward to what lies ahead, I press on toward the goal to win the [supreme and heavenly] prize to which God in Christ Jesus is calling us upward.

Philippians 3:13–14 AMPC

Forgetting the past and pressing toward the future was clearly important to Paul. He knew that feeling guilty over past mistakes would only keep him from moving forward. After he became a follower of Christ, I can only imagine how he must have felt when he thought about how he had persecuted the church and thrown Christians into jail (Acts 8:3). Following his conversion on the road to Damascus, he began to preach the same message he had condemned others for preaching (Acts 9:1–31). I am sure the devil reminded him often of his past behavior and tried to hold him back by making him feel guilty and condemned. But Paul stood firm against it.

What about Peter? Three times he denied even knowing Christ. When he realized what he had done, he went out and wept bitterly (Luke 22:54–62). This was his time of repentance, and God graciously forgave him and changed him from a coward into someone who spoke boldly on behalf of God's kingdom. On the day of Pentecost, Peter preached about Jesus, and about three thousand people were added to the church that day (Acts 2:38–41).

Some of our worst mistakes teach us the greatest lessons of our lives. Once we've made them, we simply need to learn from them, let them go, and keep working with God to follow what is in our hearts. That's how we discover the right path to our God-given destiny.

2

Success God's Way

The best things are never arrived at in haste. God is in no hurry; His plans are never rushed.

Michael R. Phillips[2]

To find the pathway to success, we must look to Scripture. Joshua 1:8 says, "Keep this Book of the Law always on your lips; meditate on it day and night, so that you may be careful to do everything written in it. Then you will be prosperous and successful."

Like most people, I spent years wanting to be successful, but initially my motivation was partially wrong. I wanted to serve God, but I also wanted to be successful because my father, who sexually abused me, often said I would never amount to anything without him. I wanted to show him he was wrong and that he was the last person on earth I needed in order to be successful. I wanted to be successful to prove I had worth and value, so it took a while for God to purify my motives. You may think you are ready to be successful now, but God knows best, and if you wait on Him, you will eventually be glad you did.

Albert Einstein said, "Try not to become a man of success. Rather become a man of value."[3] I really like this quotation because most of us want to feel successful in life without realizing that God's idea of success is more about our character, integrity, and value than about our accomplishments.

I was once a driven person, trying to succeed for many of the wrong reasons. After years of learning through my mistakes and studying God's Word, I have become a woman who seeks to succeed at being a person of character and value who walks in love, who pleases God, and is led by the Holy Spirit. I think it's good for all of us to ask ourselves, "Am I driven or am I led?"

Ask yourself, "Am I driven or am I led?"

I have read that many of the world's leaders and celebrities were abused as children. Why would this be the case? The article said they became successful because they were driven to prove they had worth and value.

Stop for a moment and think about all the so-called successful people who will have to face God one day and give an account of their lives (Romans 14:12). How shocked will they be to learn that without Jesus they are not a success, no matter what else they do?

GOD USES PEOPLE THE WORLD
WOULD IGNORE

Before I continue writing about how to be successful, I want to share some information about my background and the mental and emotional state I was in when I first began my journey with God. I think this will encourage you as you realize that God heals and uses people the world would ignore or discard.

When I was eighteen years old, I began working in the bookkeeping department of a paint business and was doing quite well. But then I met and married a young man who grew up in a dysfunctional household, as I did. He had many personality problems and character flaws, and he was a thief and a liar. He rarely worked, and he conned everyone he knew, including me, out of anything he could get. Although I was his wife, he cheated on me with other women.

Why did I marry him? Because I was desperate, afraid no one would ever want me because I had been sexually abused. Desperate people do desperate things, and that is unwise. When I look back, I realize I didn't have peace about marrying him, but because I wasn't accustomed to following the Holy Spirit, I just did whatever I wanted to do. Much of the time, it got me in trouble.

Desperate people do desperate things.

The young man I married was as dysfunctional as I was, if not more so, and the marriage was doomed from the beginning. He abandoned me several times, but I was so desperate to be loved because of the way I was raised that I foolishly took him back, only to go through the same cycle again. We were legally married for five years but were separated more than we lived together. I got pregnant, had a miscarriage, and then got pregnant again several months later. That time, he left me, lived with another woman, and told people the baby I was carrying was not his. As soon as I gave birth, he showed up at the hospital, and our son looked so much like him there was no denying he was the baby's father.

We left the hospital homeless. We literally had no

place to go, so my husband called his brother's ex-wife, who was a Christian, and asked if we could stay with her temporarily. Thankfully, she welcomed us into her home. We had no money, and she helped us as much as she could.

My husband didn't bother to work, so as soon as I was able, I found a good office job and saved enough money to rent a small apartment. Then my husband disappeared once again. Before long, he returned, and of course, I took him back. But he had a girlfriend on the side. Finally, I couldn't take any more of his lies, emotional abuse, and unfaithfulness, so I told him to leave. I filed for divorce and also had to file for bankruptcy so I would not be held responsible for his debts.

At that time, I only had one option—a bad one. I had to ask my father if I could come back and live at home. This was the last thing I wanted to do because I knew it would mean trying to stay away from his abuse, but I was desperate. I needed help with my baby and didn't make enough money to provide for us properly, and felt I had no choice but to subject myself to the possibility of being abused again.

Soon after moving back to my parents' house, I met

Dave Meyer. Meeting him was a divine intervention in my life. I had named my baby David, after my brother, and then I met Dave. I think God had a plan! I believed in God and prayed a lot during that time in my life. I asked God to get me out of the terrible situation I was in, and I constantly prayed that someday He would send me someone who would really love me. During that time, Dave was praying for a wife and asked God to give him someone who needed help. And boy, did I need help!

Dave and I had five dates. Then he asked me to marry him, and I said yes. The biggest problem was that even though I said yes, I had no idea what love was. All the people who had previously told me they loved me had either abused me or abandoned me. I had never truly been loved and had to learn what love is. God taught me about love, but it did take quite a while for me to truly believe that He loved me, that Dave loved me, and that I was worth loving.

Dave is a wonderful, godly man who truly loves me and always has. But I did not know how to receive love or how to love anyone else. We had three very rough years, and then we had several difficult years, but they were a little better than the first three. We went to church, and I loved God, but I had no idea how to successfully live the Christian life. Each night I knelt by my bed and asked God to make me a good wife, a good mother, and, most of all, a good Christian, and to forgive me for my sins. That was basically all I knew to pray. However, God saw my heart, and He had a plan for my life, just as He has a plan for yours.

GOD CHANGED ME

Although Dave and I went to church, I needed something more. I was never happy or content no matter what I was doing. One morning in 1976, on my way to work, I cried out to God, saying, "You have to do something. I can't go on like this." I felt I had come to the end of myself and my own efforts as I tried to change myself. That day, on my way home from work, God suddenly touched me and filled me with the Holy Spirit. I felt as though He had poured liquid love into me. Everything suddenly became beautiful. Even weeds were beautiful to me because I knew God made them. I didn't really know what had happened to me, but through listening to other people's testimonies on the radio, I realized people all over the world were having the same experience.

At the leading of the Holy Spirit, I started teaching a Bible study in my home, which I mentioned in the previous chapter. That was the beginning of my ministry. Ten years passed before God made clear to me that Dave and I were to start the ministry we have today. But Joyce Meyer Ministries didn't start as it is now. It started as a tiny organization and has grown over a period of thirty-seven years, as of the writing of this book. And I have had the privilege of teaching God's Word now for forty-seven years. Please remember this, so you don't become discouraged if your dream takes longer to come true than you think it should.

Apart from God's grace and enabling power, I had no qualifications to teach the Bible except that I really loved the Lord, felt led to teach His Word, and wanted to do anything He wanted me to do. If you don't feel qualified to do something you believe God is calling you to do, you are probably just the person He wants to use. He doesn't always call people who are able, but He does call those who make themselves available.

I felt I was too messed up myself to help others, but as I studied what God's Word says about the areas in which I needed help, I shared what I was learning with the few people I was teaching in my home. I discovered that most of us have the same problems in varying degrees, so the people who came to hear me teach learned as I was learning. We all learned together.

The thing about success is that you have to take an initial step, and it's often the most difficult one to take. God rarely shows us what to do all at once; He does it little by little, step by step. As we are obedient to take the first step, He then gives us the next one. He may not show it to us right away, but He will give it to us at the right time.

The first step is often the most difficult.

Looking back, I truly have no idea how I had the courage to start a Bible study or why I thought anyone would come to it. But when God calls us to do something, He opens the doors and makes the impossible possible (Matthew 19:26). He also gives us the gift of faith, which enables us to believe we can do what we otherwise would not believe we could do. We may even do things that look ridiculous to others, but it is important to listen to God rather than to people.

I started in ministry in 1976, and now I am a success, God's way. I am on television around the world on over 240 stations, and my *Enjoying Everyday Life* program is translated into more than 105 different languages. My teaching is also broadcast on over 370 radio stations. And I have written more than 140 books over the years I have been in ministry. People are changing because of God's Word, and I am happy because helping others is what makes us happy.

At Joyce Meyer Ministries, we are privileged to do many mission outreaches. I have taken sixty-seven mission trips throughout the years. My son and grandson, along with eight of our other employees, are on a mission trip in Africa right now, as I write this book. Our mission outreaches are very important to me because God's Word instructs us to help the poor, the weak, the fatherless, and those who are needy (Psalm 82:3; Proverbs 14:31), and I take this directive very seriously.

As of the writing of this book, we have published books in 161 languages and distributed over 41 million books around the world. We have helped people in the wake of over 200 natural disasters throughout the years and have served more than 479 million meals to date through our feeding programs worldwide. We have ministered to more than 3 million medical and dental patients and established more than 2,000 water wells in villages that had no clean, safe water in over 40 countries.

I share these details only to give glory to God, not to brag about myself. I also use them as an example to inspire you to believe that you can do something too. Nothing our ministry has done would have been possible unless God had ordained and maintained it. He has given us wonderful partners who financially and prayerfully support the ministry, especially in the area of missions. These people are gifts from God to us, and they are part of everything God allows us to do. We couldn't do anything we do had God not raised them up to help us. You can imagine how much money it takes to pay for everything we do, yet we have no debt and have never borrowed money.

God provides through people who want to share the gospel message about Jesus and help people who are hurting.

My story is pretty amazing, considering that I started with twelve people in a Bible study that met in my home once a week. Even that was a step of total faith, because I had no idea how to teach the Bible, but I had such a strong desire to do it that I believed I could. I studied the Bible for hours just to get one message to share each week. Although I've had no professional training, I have gone to the school of the Holy Spirit, and He has taught me well.

Every time a door opened for me to teach God's Word more, I was excited. I studied hard and did the best I could, but I always worried whether I had the right message and whether I delivered it properly. I needed more confidence in God—in His faithfulness and the ability He had given me to do what He was leading me to do. It took me a few years, but with time and experience, I finally learned to trust God every step of the way. And now, even if I make a mistake, I believe God will work it out for good in my life.

You can do seemingly impossible things with God on your side.

I will continue my story later in the book, but for now I simply want you to know that you can do amazing things—seemingly impossible things—with God on your side. You may be highly educated or not educated much at all; you may be naturally talented or feel that you have no special abilities of any kind. But whatever you feel led to do in life, the only way you can succeed God's way is to lean entirely on Him.

SELF-EFFORT OR FAITH?

For years, I worked hard in the ministry, but I didn't take time to enjoy it. I was so concerned about whether I was doing and saying the right things that I was under stress most of the time. Sometimes we do the right thing, but we do it in the wrong way or in the wrong timing. We have lessons to learn, but we finally discover that God has invited us to enter His rest (Hebrews 4:1). This is the only way we can enjoy what we are doing.

God's rest is not rest from *work but rest* **while** *we work.*

We enter God's supernatural rest by believing what He says in His Word. It is not a rest in which we take a nap or sit down for an hour. The rest of God is not rest *from* work but rest *while* we work. It has no room for worry, anxiety, or excessive reasoning. Once I learned this lesson, I started to thoroughly enjoy my assignment from God. Resting in God means I depend on Him to give me favor with the people I stand in front of instead of feeling that I must impress them. I study diligently but depend on God to make my sermons fruitful. I don't depend on myself. I choose what I think God wants me to teach, and I study and pray, then I turn it over to Him to make it turn out well. There are still times when, after teaching, I feel my sermon was terrible, but Dave and others always assure me it was great. I have learned to believe the messages are good even if I didn't feel they were at the time. I think God withholds feelings from us at certain times to teach us to walk by faith.

Success God's way is always found in His rest, not in our self-effort and struggle. Jesus says that if we are weary and overburdened, He will give us rest (Matthew 11:28–30). God is your partner in life, which means He wants to be invited to participate in everything you do. So learn to lean on God at all times, or you will never be a success God's way.

Learn to lean on God at all times.

Remember, Jesus says, "Apart from me you can do nothing" (John 15:5). If we truly believe this, we won't waste time trying to do things in our human strength and ability. What are you struggling with? Are you trying to do something God hasn't called and gifted you to do? Have you forgotten to ask God to help you? Thankfully, this problem can be fixed with one short prayer: "Father, I am sorry for trying to do this on my own. Forgive me and please help me." Maybe you're struggling because you're doing something safe instead of venturing out in faith to do what is truly in your heart. Some people are bold enough to believe they can conquer the world, and they are the ones who do. You can be one of those people; you simply need to put your trust in God, walk by faith, and live in His rest while you're doing it—one step at a time.

Are you doing something safe instead of what is truly in your heart?

3

Your Self-Image
Affects Your Future

The worst loneliness is to not be
comfortable with yourself.
Mark Twain[4]

Before I say more about success, I believe we first need to examine how we see ourselves. If you don't have confidence and a good self-image, you will not be a success. Your self-image is the picture you carry of yourself on the inside, in your heart and mind. If you don't like yourself and you frequently find fault with yourself, you are not likely to succeed in life. Sadly, a large majority of people don't like themselves. They compare themselves with others, forgetting that those people have faults too. They may be hiding their faults and pretending to be something more than they are, but they have their struggles and shortcomings. If you want an example of someone to be like, look at Jesus, not at another human being.

You will not be a success without confidence and a good self-image.

You and I are permanently flawed, as is everyone else. But we are also fearfully and wonderfully made (Psalm 139:14). Realizing that I will always have some faults and being okay with it took me a long time. If I didn't have any faults, I wouldn't need Jesus, so now I gladly accept my weaknesses. I do ask God to help me with them, and quite often He does. But then something else is revealed, something I don't like. The truth is that we will never manifest perfection until our earthly bodies have ceased to exist and we are at home in heaven with the Lord.

We learn from 2 Corinthians 12:9 that God's grace is sufficient, and His strength is made perfect and shows itself through our weaknesses. Also in this verse, Paul writes that he learned to "boast all the more gladly about my weaknesses, so that Christ's power may rest on me."

A PERFECT HEART

Although we cannot manifest perfection in our thoughts, words, and deeds, we can have a perfect heart toward God. Thankfully, through His grace and the help of the Holy Spirit, we do gradually improve, even though we will never be perfect. We can celebrate and enjoy our progress instead of being angry with ourselves because of our imperfections.

Second Chronicles 16:9 says, "For the eyes of the Lord run to and fro throughout the whole earth, to show Himself strong on behalf of those whose heart is loyal to Him" (NKJV). This scripture encourages me because it teaches that God will show Himself strong in those whose hearts are perfect toward Him, not in those who perform perfectly. What is a perfect heart? I think it is the desire found in someone who wants to be perfect in God's sight—someone who loves God completely and wants to do His will. Although these people may have weaknesses, it does not mean they have wicked hearts. People whose hearts are perfect are grieved when they sin, but they don't waste time feeling guilty. They quickly repent, receive forgiveness, and press forward to the good things God has planned for them.

CONFIDENCE

Martin Luther said, "Faith is a living, daring confidence in God's grace, so sure and certain that a man could stake his life on it a thousand times."[5]

We don't put confidence in ourselves; we put it in Christ Jesus. Our goal is not to be self-confident or

self-reliant, but to be confident in God, who lives in
our hearts and who has promised to never leave us
and to be with us always (Deuteronomy 31:8; Matthew 28:20). He has also given us His Holy Spirit as
our helper (John 14:26). I believe I can do things, but I
know I cannot do them right without God's help. Jesus
says, "Apart from me you can do nothing" (John 15:5).
To be successful, we need to lean on God at all times,
for all things.

People who are insecure about themselves suffer
mentally, emotionally, socially, and spiritually. I know
this because I was insecure for many years and have
met thousands of others who struggle with insecurity.
Each of us has a God-given destiny and should be free
to fulfill it. But that won't happen as long as we are
insecure and have a poor self-image. To be a success
at anything, we must be willing to try things. If we try
something and it doesn't work, we should try something else. People who are insecure and have a poor
self-image don't do this because they are fearful. They
would rather do nothing and feel safe than risk trying
something new and having it not work out.

Before God formed us in the womb, He knew and

approved of us as His chosen instruments (Jeremiah 1:5 AMPC). This assures us that God has something special for each of us to do—including you. He knows every mistake you will make before you make it, and He has still chosen you. God never intends for us to fight against ourselves or not to like ourselves. He wants us to believe in and accept His unconditional love, and to let that love give us the confidence we need to succeed in every area of our lives.

God does not intend for you to fight against yourself.

RELATIONSHIPS

We all have relationships—with people, with God, and with ourselves. But we rarely think much about our relationship with ourselves, and it is vitally important. Our relationship with ourselves even affects our relationship with God and certainly influences our relationships with other people. If we are insecure and lack confidence, we project an image of timidity and weakness, and the people we are trying to be in relationship with will feel the same way about us as we feel about ourselves.

I once had a secretary who lacked confidence in almost every way. This caused me to lack confidence in her too, and eventually we were unable to work together because of it. I saw her the way she saw herself. I wanted to feel confident that she could do whatever I gave her to do, or that at least she would try her best. But I realized this would not happen because she had a poor self-image, a lot of fear, and little confidence.

The Bible tells us the story of twelve spies that Moses sent into Canaan, the Promised Land, to scout out the land and see if it was good (Numbers 13:1–14:8). When the twelve came back, ten of them gave a negative report about the giants in the land and said they knew they could not defeat them. The Amplified Bible, Classic Edition calls this "an evil report" (Numbers 13:32). Only two men, Joshua and Caleb, gave a good report full of confidence (Numbers 14:6–8). The negative spies saw the giants and said Israel could not defeat them because "we were like grasshoppers in our own sight, and so we were in their sight" (Numbers

13:33 NKJV). But the two men who had a positive attitude, Joshua and Caleb, believed the Israelites could enter the Promised Land. Only two out of twelve had confidence that they could conquer the people currently living in the land.

They told Moses, We came to the land to which you sent us; surely it flows with milk and honey. This is its fruit. But the people who dwell there are strong, and the cities are fortified and very large; moreover, there we saw the sons of Anak [of great stature and courage]. Amalek dwells in the land of the South (the Negeb); the Hittite, the Jebusite, and the Amorite dwell in the hill country; and the Canaanite dwells by the sea and along by the side of the Jordan [River]. Caleb quieted the people before Moses, and said, Let us go up at once and possess it; we are well able to conquer it. But his fellow scouts said, We are not able to go up against the people [of Canaan], for they are stronger than we are. So they brought the Israelites an evil report of the land which they had scouted out, saying, The land through which we

went to spy it out is a land that devours its inhab-
itants. And all the people that we saw in it are
men of great stature. There we saw the Nephilim
[or giants], the sons of Anak, who come from the
giants; and we were in our own sight as grasshoppers, and so we were in their sight.

Numbers 13:27–33 AMPC

This Scripture passage provides a wonderful example of how our thoughts hinder us or help us, depending on the level of our confidence. Ten of the men saw
themselves as grasshoppers (unable and incapable),
and the people they needed to defeat saw them the
same way they saw themselves.

I encourage you to honestly examine how you feel
about yourself. Be humble, not proud, but also be confident because you know God loves you and is available to help you at all times. When you succeed, thank
God. If you fail, shake it off and move on to the next
thing. We can learn from every mistake. I often say that
we fail our way to success.

I urge you to have a good relationship with yourself. Enjoy yourself, even the parts of you that are a

little quirky or unusual. Know your strengths and thank God for them, and know your weaknesses and ask God to help you with them.

It is vitally important for you to like yourself, because you are with yourself all the time. God will never help you be someone else, but He will help you be the best "you" that you can be. Be like Joshua and Caleb and say, "I can do it." Believe you are created by God, in His image (Genesis 1:27), and that everything He creates is good.

It is vitally important for you to like yourself.

THE DEVIL IS A LIAR

The devil is our enemy, and he is a liar (John 8:44). He tells us we can't do certain things when God wants us to know we can. Why would we believe a liar? We believe him because we don't know he is lying. Perhaps we have listened to his lies for so long that we are rooted in them. Jesus is the truth (John 14:6), and He is the one we should believe. Believing in Jesus means believing His Word. I am amazed at how we often find it easier to believe the devil's lies than to believe the truth. When we believe lies, we are deceived. When we are deceived, what is not true seems true to us. A lie becomes our reality.

---

*Believing in Jesus means believing
His Word.*

The Bible, God's Word, has thousands of good things to say about us. The more of them we believe, the more powerful we are, and the more likely we are to succeed in life. Romans 12:2 teaches us to be transformed by renewing our minds instead of conforming to the world's philosophies. We renew our minds by aligning our thoughts with God's Word.

Here are just ten good things God's Word says about you:

- God loves you unconditionally
  (1 John 4:9–10; Romans 5:8).

- God lives inside of you and enables you to do whatever you need to do (Romans 8:11; Philippians 4:13).
- God goes before you and is with you. He will never leave you or forsake you, so you don't need to be afraid or discouraged (Deuteronomy 31:8).
- You are fearfully and wonderfully made (Psalm 139:14).
- You have the mind of Christ (1 Corinthians 2:16).
- You are the righteousness of God in Christ (2 Corinthians 5:21).
- Your sins are forgiven (Psalm 103:10–12).
- You are created in the image of God (Genesis 1:27).
- You are more than a conqueror through Christ who loves you (Romans 8:37).
- There is no condemnation for those who are in Christ Jesus (Romans 8:1).

I strongly encourage you to know God's promises and be familiar with the good things He says about

you. The world may tell you that you will never succeed, but that is a lie. If you will simply believe the ten
biblical truths listed above, I believe you'll see your life
change in amazing ways.

Consider the apostle Paul's instructions in Romans
12:2 (AMPC):

> Do not be conformed to this world (this age),
> [fashioned after and adapted to its exter-
> nal, superficial customs], but be transformed
> (changed) by the [entire] renewal of your mind
> [by its new ideals and its new attitude], so that
> you may prove [for yourselves] what is the good
> and acceptable and perfect will of God, even the
> thing which is good and acceptable and perfect
> [in His sight for you].

To put this passage of Scripture simply, if we want
to experience the good life God has prearranged for us
to live, our minds must be renewed according to His
Word. We must learn to think as God thinks. In order
to do this, we will need to learn His Word. This will
enable us to recognize the devil's lies and to cast them

down (refuse to believe them). It was a great revelation to me to learn that many of my thoughts were planted in my mind by the devil, and that I didn't have to think and meditate on something just because it came into my mind. We can choose our thoughts.

You can choose your own thoughts.

Second Corinthians 10:4–5 says:

The weapons we fight with are not the weapons of the world. On the contrary, they have divine power to demolish strongholds. We demolish arguments and every pretension that sets itself up against the knowledge of God, and we take captive every thought to make it obedient to Christ.

It is our job, with the Holy Spirit's help, to bring our thoughts into agreement with God's Word and not just passively think anything that pops into our minds. In the beginning, this may seem hard to do, but the more you do it, the easier it becomes. Learn to think about yourself the way God thinks about you, and you will have taken the first step toward being a success.

GOD WILL MEET YOU WHERE YOU ARE

God will always meet us where we are if we ask Him to. We don't have to try to get to God; in His mercy and grace, He comes to us. We read in Genesis 21:17 (AMPC) that this happened to Hagar: "And God heard the voice of the youth, and the angel of God called to Hagar out of heaven and said to her, What troubles you, Hagar? Fear not, for God has heard the voice of the youth *where he is*" (emphasis mine).

We see in this scripture that Hagar and her son, Ishmael (referred to as "the youth"), were in trouble. But God spoke to them in the wilderness *where they were* and immediately began to help them and give them direction. When we read the Bible, we frequently find that when God's people were in trouble, He met them where they were and helped them.

God makes miracles out of your mistakes.

God delights in taking our mistakes and making miracles out of them if we ask Him to. General Colin Powell said, "There are no secrets to success. It is the result of preparation, hard work, and learning from failure."[6] I would add to this, "and seeking God in all you do, always asking for His help."

All too often when we are in trouble, we assume that God won't help us because we have made mistakes. But this isn't a biblical way to think. God knew every mistake we would ever make before we made it. Jesus is a High Priest who understands our weaknesses and infirmities because He "has been tempted in every respect as we are, yet without sinning. Let us then fearlessly and confidently and boldly draw near to the throne of grace (the throne of God's unmerited favor to us sinners), that we may receive mercy [for our failures] and find grace to help in good time for every need" (Hebrews 4:15–16 AMPC). Notice we are to come to the throne "boldly." This means we approach God with confidence that He is faithful, and that when He says He will do something, we can know for certain that He will do it. He may not do it immediately, but He will do it.

As I mentioned earlier, my father sexually abused me for years, starting when I was very young. The abuse I suffered was definitely wrong. It should not have happened to me, but the devil was controlling my father, and I got hurt as a result. However, God took that terrible thing and turned it into my message, my ministry, and my miracle. He has allowed me to use what Satan meant for harm to help many other people (Genesis 50:20). Nothing is too hard for God (Jeremiah 32:17). You have not made so many mistakes in the past that you are beyond becoming successful in the future. God loves you unconditionally and is just waiting for you to ask for His help.

God is waiting for you to ask for His help.

I prayed many times and asked God to get me out of the abusive situation when I was growing up, but He didn't. However, He did get me through it, and that has helped me become the person I am today. I tried on several occasions to get help, but no one wanted to intervene. I told my mother, but she was afraid of my father and of the scandal that would result if anyone found out what he was doing. I told my aunt and uncle, and they didn't want to get involved. I asked my dad to stop doing what he was doing and told him how it made me feel, and he became so angry I thought he was going to injure me. You may wonder, as I did for a long time, why God didn't deliver me sooner. But I no longer question this. Instead, I look at the good that has come from it, and I leave the unanswered questions with God, where they belong.

God is our Redeemer, and He is the God of justice. He makes wrong things right. I have seen Him do this in my life and the lives of thousands of other people, and He will do the same for you.

God makes wrong things right.

First Corinthians 1:27 says, "But God has chosen the foolish things of the world to put to shame the wise, and God has chosen the weak things of the world to put to shame the things which are mighty" (NKJV). I conclude from this verse that God purposefully chooses the most unlikely candidates for the jobs He wants us to do. By doing so, He shows His grace, mercy, and power to change human lives. When God uses someone like me or you or many other people, we realize that the source of our success is not in ourselves but in God. Other people notice this too.

Each of us has a destiny, and there is no reason for us not to fulfill it, unless we listen to and believe the devil's lies. We can't use weakness as an excuse because God is ready to give us all the strength we need. We can't use our sinful past as an excuse because God has forgiven us and set us free. Just think of the apostle Paul, formerly known as Saul. Before his miraculous transformation, he persecuted Christians and searched for them so he could put them in prison (Acts 8:3). But Jesus appeared to him and said He was going to use him (Acts 9:1–6). Or what about Peter, who denied three times that he even knew Jesus (Luke 22:54–62) yet he became one of the greatest apostles. These examples show us that it is not how God sees us that is a problem; it is how we see ourselves. Each of us can succeed at everything God intends for us to do if we simply realize we cannot do it alone. We need God's help at all times. We simply need to ask Him to help us and be patient as He works in our lives.

The problem is not how God sees you but how you see yourself.

Spend some quiet time alone and take an inventory of how you feel about yourself. How do you see yourself? Do you believe God is greater than your failures and weaknesses?

One key to success is to never give up. God has a new and wonderful life waiting for you, a life filled with success. All you need to do is believe this and then begin to apply the principles you learn in this book and others, including the Bible. Do you believe you can succeed with God's help? If you believe it, it can happen. But if you don't believe it, it won't.

4

Keeping God First

*Don't seek opportunity, seek God, and then
opportunity will seek you.*

Mark Batterson[7]

I had been a Christian for a long time before I was taught the importance of seeking God for Himself rather than for what I wanted Him to do for me. We need Him more than we need anything else; and I have finally learned that if I seek Him first, He will give me everything I need and many things I want, unless they are not part of His will for me. If you truly want to be successful God's way, it is necessary to keep Him first in all things. Psalm 37:4 says, *"Delight yourself also in the Lord, and He will give you the desires and secret petitions of your heart"* (AMPC, emphasis mine).

Keep God first in all things.

Many people in the world appear to be very successful. They have a lot of money, they own many things, and they have power because of their positions. But I don't consider them to be successful God's way. Many of them are rarely happy, and some have been found to be dishonest or to lack other moral virtues. They often take credit for their accomplishments and refer to themselves as "self-made." Always remember that no matter how much money people have or how famous they are, if they don't have Jesus in their life, they really have nothing at all.

When people are successful God's way, they know their success is due to God's grace and goodness in their lives, and they give Him the credit He is due. They also thank Him frequently for what He has done for them. A successful life is filled with thanksgiving and gratitude. Think about this: What if you woke up today and all you had was what you were thankful for yesterday? We should always remember and be thankful for all God's goodness in our lives.

God says through the prophet Jeremiah, "My people have committed two sins: They have forsaken me, the spring of living water, and have dug their own cisterns, broken cisterns that cannot hold water" (Jeremiah 2:13). This describes perfectly what we do when we forget God. We start to try to make our own way, but we find it empty. We bring our problems on ourselves by forsaking God (Jeremiah 2:17). Perhaps one of the saddest scriptures in the Bible is Jeremiah 2:32, when God says, "My people have forgotten me, days without number."

God should be the first person we think of in the morning and the first one we talk to. From Genesis to Revelation, Scripture urges us to seek God. *Seek* is a strong word that means to crave, pursue, and go after with all your strength. It means to require and to be unwilling to do without. People who seek God study His Word and educate themselves concerning the things of God.

The Bible tells us to love the Lord with all our heart, soul, mind, and strength (Mark 12:30). It doesn't instruct us to go to church for an hour each week and not think of God until the next Sunday. God wants to be involved in every aspect of our lives. We should talk to Him and listen to Him all the time.

When people don't keep God first in their lives, they often lack some provision and don't enjoy the provision they do have because they worry about losing it. They may also lack peace and joy, and feel depressed, discouraged, and discontent. They may have relational problems or substance abuse issues. They don't tend to feel good about themselves, so they try to use money, possessions, position, and worldly power to give them the worth and value only God can give.

During Old Testament times, people lived under the

law (God's ceremonial, civil and moral requirements). Jesus came to fulfill the law—a law we could never obey but Jesus fully obeyed on our behalf (Matthew 5:17; 2 Corinthians 5:21). Unlike the Old Testament sacrificial system that provided temporary forgiveness of sins, Jesus' death on the cross became the final sacrifice that completely paid the price for all our sins. When He died on the cross, He said, "It is finished" (John 19:30). I believe He was referring to the law. God's moral law is still applicable under the New Covenant, which we now live under in Christ, but we follow His moral code because we know He loves us, we love Him, and we want to serve and obey Him. We don't do it to get anything from God, but to please Him because He has given us so much.

There is no point in saying God is first in our lives if we put everything else before Him. Put Him first in your money, in your time, and in all your decisions. This isn't difficult, and you don't have to be on your knees constantly praying about the right thing to do. If you truly want God's will, you can pray and go about your life, trusting that God will interrupt you if you are not going in the direction He wants you to go.

Matthew 6:33 says, "But seek first the kingdom of

God and His righteousness, and all these things shall be added to you" (NKJV). And 1 John 5:21 teaches us to keep ourselves from idols, meaning that we must diligently avoid anything that occupies the place in our hearts that belongs to God. An idol is not merely a stone or wooden statue to which people bow down. Anything can be an idol when it becomes more important in your life than God. Your career can become your idol. Your home and how it looks can be so important to you that it begins to crowd out God. You can idolize other people, such as a boyfriend or girlfriend, a spouse, or your children. The temptation and danger of not keeping God in first place are constant. Satan is always trying to push Him out of our lives, and we must be determined to keep Him in first place.

Anything can become an idol if it becomes more important in your life than God.

One of the drawbacks of success can be that we get so busy we don't have time for God anymore. Satan will even use the things God gives you to draw you away from Him. God gave me the ministry I have, but there was a time when He rightly chastised me for spending most of my time doing ministry and very little time with Him. Working for God should not take the place of spending time with Him. If your dream is to own your own business, and God brings that to pass, don't fall into the trap of spending all your time on your business and only giving God the leftovers, if anything at all. Put Him first at all times, and you will succeed beyond anything you can imagine.

Working for God should not replace spending time with Him.

Give God the first portion of every day. You can do this by praying, reading the Bible, or by absorbing His Word through some of the amazing ways technology provides, including television, radio, apps, and podcasts. In addition to reading and studying your Bible, I highly recommend reading other good books that will help you grow in your love and understanding of God's Word.

I realize some people have more time than others, but whatever amount you have, give God the first portion, and you will be amazed at how things will change in your life. If you can only spend five minutes in the morning, consider taking some of your lunchtime and giving it to God or spending time with Him before bed. There is always a way to do what we need to do if we want it strongly enough.

One of the best ways to examine your priorities is to ask yourself what you spend most of your free time doing. If you watch television for four hours in the evenings, television is a priority to you. If you have that much time to watch TV, surely you can find a little time to spend with God. By giving God the first portion of everything, you become "qualified to be multiplied," meaning that He will take what you give Him and give you more of everything else you need.

Give God the first portion of everything.

ACKNOWLEDGE GOD

Proverbs 3:5–7 (AMPC) is a wonderful Scripture passage that reminds us to include God in all we do:

> Lean on, trust in, and be confident in the Lord with all your heart and mind and do not rely on your own insight or understanding. In all your ways know, recognize, and acknowledge Him, and He will direct and make straight and plain your paths. Be not wise in your own eyes; reverently fear and worship the Lord and turn [entirely] away from evil.

As you'll discover in a later chapter, your thoughts and mind have a lot to do with your success or lack of it. Therefore, we trust God not only in our hearts, but also in our minds. My favorite part of Proverbs 3:5–7 is in verse 6, which teaches us to "acknowledge" God in all our ways. This means to pay attention to Him, to share our plans with Him, and to let Him know that if He doesn't approve of any of them, we will make whatever changes He wants. This is the respectful thing to do. It means we don't want to do anything that does not have God's approval. Talking to and listening for God throughout the day is a wonderful habit to form. He created us for fellowship with Him. Whisper several times a day, "I love You, Lord. Thank You for all You do for me."

"Thank You, Lord, for all You do for me."

GOD'S PRESENCE

God says He will never leave us or forsake us, but that He will be with us always (Joshua 1:9). God will guide us, but we need to ask Him to do so (James 4:2). We should learn to seek God for His presence, not His presents, meaning the blessings He can give us. When God revealed this to me many years ago, it was life-changing. Think of it this way: I love it when my children drop by my house just to see me. I also love to give to them, but if they only came around when I had presents for them, I would feel used, not loved.

The psalmist David writes:

One thing have I asked of the Lord, that will I seek, inquire for, and [insistently] require: that I may dwell in the house of the Lord [in His presence] all the days of my life, to behold and gaze upon the beauty [the sweet attractiveness and the delightful loveliness] of the Lord and to meditate, consider, and inquire in His temple.

Psalm 27:4 AMPC

Making the transition from wanting God's presents to wanting His presence is a sign of spiritual maturity. God is never more than one thought away, so you don't have to try to find Him. He is with you always. Simply acknowledge Him in all things, and you will begin to feel closer to Him. In Psalm 51:11, David cries out to God not to take His presence from him. I pray this will always be the cry of my heart and yours.

James 4:4–5 says:

You adulterous people, don't you know that friendship with the world means enmity against

God? Therefore, anyone who chooses to be a friend of the world becomes an enemy of God. Or do you think Scripture says without reason that he jealously longs for the spirit he has caused to dwell in us?

These are strong words. God is jealous of anything or anyone we put before Him. He says that anyone who loves the world cannot love Him. He wants to be your first love. We are created for God (Revelation 4:11), and we belong to Him. I am so glad I belong to Him; aren't you?

I heard someone say that "God is either Lord *of* all, or He is not Lord *at* all." We know that He is Lord of all. Jesus redeemed us. He purchased us with His blood, and we no longer belong to ourselves, according to 1 Corinthians 6:19–20 (AMPC):

God is either Lord of *all, or He is not Lord* at *all.*

Do you not know that your body is the temple (the very sanctuary) of the Holy Spirit Who lives within you, Whom you have received [as a Gift] from God? You are not your own, you were bought with a price [purchased with a preciousness and paid for, made His own]. So then, honor God and bring glory to Him in your body.

Christ lives in you. You cannot get any closer to anyone than that. Think of this often, and it will help you be more conscious and aware of His presence.

Christ lives in you.

SEEK GOD AS MUCH IN GOOD TIMES AS IN HARD TIMES

It is amazing how quickly we can find time to pray and seek God when we are in need, but we don't seem to have much, if any, time for Him when everything is going well for us. God is not available for emergencies only. He is available for everything, all the time.

God tested the Israelites to see if they would keep His commandments in the wilderness (Deuteronomy 8:2). He warned them not to forget Him when they had everything they wanted:

> Beware that you do not forget the Lord your God by not keeping His commandments, His precepts, and His statutes which I command you today, lest when you have eaten and are full, and have built goodly houses and live in them, and when your herds and flocks multiply and your silver and gold is multiplied and all you have is multiplied, then your [minds and] hearts be lifted up and you forget the Lord your God, Who brought you out of the land of Egypt, out of the house of bondage.
>
> Deuteronomy 8:11–14 AMPC

In this passage, Moses urges the Israelites, once things get better, not to forget where they came from and not to forget God, who gave them their blessings.

I think we can all use a regular reminder of the importance of keeping God in first place in our lives.

Jesus says, "If you [really] love Me, you will keep (obey) My commands" (John 14:15 AMPC). Obedience often requires personal sacrifice, but if God asks us to give up something, we may eventually realize it wasn't good for us anyway, or He may replace it with something much more wonderful than what we gave up. When we have God in our lives, we can always be satisfied. Paul said he knew how to be content when he had an abundance and when he didn't, in good times or in hard times (Philippians 4:11–12).

When Jesus suffered His agony in the garden of Gethsemane, He prayed three separate times, asking God to take away the cup of suffering He was being asked to drink, referring to the crucifixion (Matthew 26:39, 42, 44). Each time, He closed His prayer by asking for God's will to be done over His own. Jesus did not want to go to the cross and suffer as He knew He would, but He wanted to do God's will more than He wanted His own. His willingness to sacrifice has brought blessings to millions and will continue to do so.

Any sacrifice we make in obedience to God will be

rewarded many times over. Obedience to God is the primary pathway to success. Joshua 1:8 says, "Keep this Book of the Law always on your lips; meditate on it day and night, so that you may be careful to do everything written in it. Then you will be prosperous and successful." I will summarize this verse with this exhortation to you: Know the Word, do the Word, prosper, and succeed.

Obedience to God is the primary pathway to success.

THE MOST DIFFICULT TYPES OF OBEDIENCE

Sometimes being obedient is more difficult than at other times. Consider these situations when obedience is especially challenging:

- When you have no feelings to support your decisions or actions

- When you see no visible signs of progress or success
- When results seem delayed

Not only did Jesus obey God when doing so was agonizing and provide the ultimate example of surrender to God, others throughout the Bible also faced difficult circumstances when they chose to obey Him, and they were eventually blessed:

- Noah built the ark when no one had ever seen rain (Genesis 6:9–22).
- Esther approached the king uninvited when the punishment for doing so was death, unless he held out the golden scepter to her (Esther 4:11; 5:2).
- Elisha left everything to follow Elijah (1 Kings 19:19–21).
- Abram left his home and family and went to an unknown place (Genesis 12:1).
- The disciples left everything behind to follow Jesus (Matthew 19:27–29).

- Abraham prepared to sacrifice Isaac
  (Genesis 22:1–14).

People who do great things make great sacrifices.
Would you be willing to make a great sacrifice to see
your dreams come to pass? When I went into the ministry, I had to leave my life as I knew it. I lost most of my
friends, because in those days it was uncommon, and
in many circles unacceptable, for women to teach the
Bible or preach. But if any of the people who rejected
me are still around, I believe they can see that God was
right and they were wrong. People often fear what they
don't understand or aren't familiar with, and although
the rejection hurt me, I understand that it was hard for
them to understand and accept what I was doing.

People who do great things make
great sacrifices.

When you believe that God is speaking to
your heart, letting you know that He is going to do

something special in your life, it is usually best to keep it to yourself and let the proof be the convincing factor.

As I close this chapter, I want to remind you once more to always keep God first in your life. As you do, He will take care of everything else that needs to be done or show you what to do and give you the strength to do it.

5

☙

Your Thoughts and Words Affect Your Success

☙

Change your thoughts and you change your world.

Norman Vincent Peale[8]

Our thoughts are the seeds of what we want to see happen in the future. Thoughts produce words, and both our thoughts and our words are important. Learning about the power of thoughts and words changed my life. What is the point in thinking and speaking something negative when you can choose to think and say something positive, creative, and filled with life? What is the point in praying that God will give you success in your new business and then speaking about it as though it will never happen? Sometimes we pray for good things to happen, then talk about how afraid we are that they never will. This is not a recipe for success.

Build a successful image inside yourself by thinking thoughts that will help you, not hinder you. See yourself as successful. Believe you will be successful. And spend time with people who will encourage you, not discourage you. Make a priority of being around successful people.

David prayed, "May these words of my mouth and this meditation of my heart be pleasing in your sight, Lord, my Rock and my Redeemer" (Psalm 19:14). We would be wise to pray that our words and meditations (thoughts) are pleasing to God too.

When I looked up how many thoughts the average person has per day, the results varied, but the most common answer was approximately six thousand. That's a lot of thoughts. Just imagine how your life would change if you thought six thousand positive thoughts about your future rather than six thousand negative ones. Thoughts rush through our minds like a speeding train. Most of the time we don't even realize what we are thinking, but we can change this. We must have our minds renewed according to God's Word. In other words, we need to learn to think as God thinks. I know this is possible, because prior to learning how powerful our thoughts were, probably 5,900 of mine were negative. When I realized this and knew it needed to change, I began to think more optimistically.

Changing my thinking took time, effort, and a lot of prayer and study of God's Word, but now I am a very positive person. Also, I no longer like being around negative people who talk only about their problems or the troubles in the world. Part of what is wrong with our world today is that people are extremely negative, and the news is filled with stories of all the bad things that are happening. Rarely do we hear or read a story from the news media that makes us feel good. Just imagine how many negative thoughts and words go out into the atmosphere in today's society. No wonder the world's problems keep getting worse.

Romans 4:17 says that God "calls those things which do not exist as though they did" (NKJV). If you have a dream for your life, I encourage you to take a moment to close your eyes and see it happening. God has given us an imagination, so why not use it for good things? Think about your dream as though it has already become a reality, and talk about it as though you firmly believe it is on its way to you. When I began to believe that God would use me to teach His Word around the world, I made lists of Scripture-based statements to confess aloud and lists of things to think about and pray about. I did this for a long time before I saw any of my dreams manifest, but eventually they did.

---

*Close your eyes and see your
dreams happening.*

The power of God can be released and a person's life can be turned around through the right words at the right time (Proverbs 25:11). In the Old Testament, Job says, "How forceful are right words!" (Job 6:25 NKJV). I believe words are forceful indeed. Just think about the power of your words. How many times have you made someone happy by saying the right thing? And how many times have you made someone sad or damaged a relationship by saying the wrong thing? Words have power. Are your thoughts and words in agreement with God's Word and with what you believe He wants to do in your life? If the answer is yes, great. But if not, you can begin to change that right now. You can choose what you want to think about. Satan will work hard to put life-draining thoughts instead of life-giving ones into your mind, but you can learn to refuse negative thoughts and replace them with positive ones.

You can choose what you want to think about.

Romans 12:3 reminds us of an important truth: "For by the grace given me I say to every one of you: Do not think of yourself more highly than you ought, but rather think of yourself with sober judgment, in accordance with the faith God has distributed to each of you."

While we are waiting for our dreams and goals to become realities, we should tell the Lord that we know they can only happen if He makes them happen, and that we know we are nothing without Him.

THE WAITING TIME

Jesus says in Mark 11:24, "Therefore I tell you, whatever you ask for in prayer, believe that you have received it, and it will be yours." He does not tell us how long we will have to wait. You may wonder how you can believe you have received something if you can't see or touch it yet. This is where faith comes in. Faith is the evidence of things we don't see, the proof of their reality (Hebrews 11:1). After we ask God for something according to His will, our faith becomes a title deed to it. I could show you the deed to my home, and you would definitely believe I owned a house, even though you could not see it. Faith works the same way.

Waiting in fear and worry will make you miserable and keep you from seeing what you are waiting for. Standing firm in faith is the key to possessing your request.

Faith has its own thoughts and language. As we wait for our prayers to be answered or our dreams to come true, our faith is tested. During this waiting period, it is important to think and speak words that exercise faith, not fear, worry, doubt, or unbelief. Even when you don't see anything happening, say, "God is working. My breakthrough is on its way," or "Something good is going to happen to me today."

Our faith is tested while we wait for our prayers to be answered.

Paul writes about himself, "I have fought the good fight, I have finished the race, I have kept the faith" (2 Timothy 4:7). I want to be able to speak these words about myself, and I hope you do too. Sometimes we have to fight to hold on to our faith. We battle doubt, negative thoughts, the temptation to give up, and many other things. When ungodly thoughts bombard my mind, I find that speaking God's Word aloud is the best way to get rid of them.

When the devil tells you that nothing will ever change and you will not get what you ask for, answer him with a scripture, as Jesus did when He was in the wilderness for forty days while the devil tempted and lied to Him. Each time the devil lied, Jesus responded, "It is written," or, "It is said," and He quoted a scripture to refute the lie (Luke 4:4, 8,12).

Fight the good fight of faith. Don't stand by and let the devil win. According to Romans 8:37, you are more than a conqueror through Christ, which means God has already given you victory over the enemy.

People who believe they can do what has never been done before are the ones who do it. The only limits on you are the ones you put on yourself unless you are trying to do something that isn't God's will for you.

*Believe you can do what has never been
done before.*

God is never in a hurry. Rarely do great things happen quickly. If they do, many of them fall apart. We must have a strong foundation before we build a house (Matthew 7:24), because although foundations are not exciting, they are crucial if we want to build something that will last. Anyone who wants to be a success cannot be in a hurry because God grows us gradually and promotes us little by little.

*You can't be in a hurry if you want to
be a success.*

During the years I was waiting to see growth and make progress in my ministry, my faith was tested over and over again. But my testimony is "I am still here, and I have what I asked for and waited for." I have a testimony of victory, not failure, and you will too if you decide you will never give up on the dream God has given you.

THE MIND OF THE SPIRIT

Romans 8:5–6 says, "Those who live according to the flesh have their minds set on what the flesh desires; but those who live in accordance with the Spirit have their minds set on what the Spirit desires. The mind governed by the flesh is death, but the mind governed by the Spirit is life and peace."

If you lose your peace or joy, just examine what you have been thinking about, and you will probably find the source of your problem. Most likely, your thoughts led you to feel disturbed, uneasy, or sad. You were thinking with the mind of the flesh instead of the mind of the Spirit. If you truly want to have success, think according to what you want, not according to what you have. Where our minds go, we follow. So if you want success, think thoughts of success. If you think successful thoughts, you will speak successful words, and this will build a successful image in your heart.

Think according to what you want,
not what you have.

A lot of the things God asks us to do don't make sense to our natural minds, apart from the influence and guidance of the Holy Spirit. Romans 8:7 says, "The mind governed by the flesh is hostile to God; it does not submit to God's law, nor can it do so." I have already mentioned how little sense it made for me to be in ministry from a natural perspective, but the Holy Spirit makes sense out of things that seem senseless to us. He enables us to do things we could never do without Him. Maybe you have a dream that is too big for you. That doesn't mean that it is too big for God. Remember, all things are possible with Him (Matthew 19:26).

ADVICE FROM PEOPLE
WHO SUCCEEDED

Many people throughout history have achieved success, some of them against tremendous odds. I've chosen some advice I think will help you as you endeavor to succeed.

1. Dream big.

I would rather dream big and get part of what I hope for than to dream small and get all of it.

Better to dream big and get some of what you want than dream small and get all of it.

Michelangelo said, "The greater danger for most of us is not in setting our aim too high and falling short but in setting our aim too short and reaching it."[9]

2. Stay positive.

Thomas Jefferson declared, "Nothing can stop the man with the right mental attitude from achieving his goal; nothing on earth can help the man with the wrong mental attitude."[10]

3. Work hard.

J. C. Penney, who founded JCPenney department stores, said, "Unless you are willing to drench yourself in your work beyond the capacity of the average man, you are just not cut out for positions at the top."[11]

4. Turn failure into a fresh start.

The Roman statesman Seneca, said: "Every new beginning comes from some other beginning's end."[12]

5. Learn to get along well with other people.

According to former US president Theodore Roosevelt, "The most important single ingredient in the formula of success is knowing how to get along with people."[13]

EVERY PROBLEM HAS AN ANSWER

Are problems stopping you from becoming a success? They don't have to. If you will believe this too, problems will not hinder your progress. I firmly believe that every problem has an answer. You can begin to solve the problems you face if you will begin to think and speak differently about them.

God's Word has an answer to every problem.

There is no point in believing you can be a success without becoming a problem-solver. I believe God's Word contains an answer to every problem we could ever face—if not an exact answer, at least a principle or truth that will lead to the answers we need. The Holy Spirit is our helper, and if we turn to Him to help us solve our problems, He will. He lives in every believer, so trust Him to guide you in the right direction when you need wisdom.

I can say without a doubt that the Holy Spirit has never failed to give me the help I need when I need it. It may not come until the last minute, but He is faithful.

When I started my first Bible study at the church I attended, we needed space to provide a nursery for the children. The church rented space for the Sunday and midweek services, but the women's ministry had no money to cover the cost of a nursery during the Bible study. We prayed, asking God to reveal where we could minister to the children, and He showed us an unused mobile home on the church property. It worked perfectly for us. The amazing thing is that it was sitting in front of us the entire time. We simply didn't think of it as the right place for a nursery. We had a problem, and God had an answer.

The Holy Spirit has never failed to give me the help I need.

About ten years later, Dave and I needed a building for our ministry. We had looked and looked and had been unable to find anything. One day, on our daily drive to our rented office space, we noticed a road that led to fifty-five acres of property with a small for sale sign on it. We had never thought to drive up the road and see what was there. When we looked at it, we realized it would meet our needs perfectly and bought it for a reasonable price. Our ministry buildings are still on this property today. I believe that God often hides things from us until the time is just right for Him to reveal them.

During forty-five years of ministry, we have faced a lot of problems, but we have never been left without an answer. If you have a problem screaming at you right now, just remember that God is faithful and has just the right answer for you.

I believe it's difficult to overestimate the impact of thoughts and words on success. Think about the people you view as successful. I'm sure they don't think and speak negatively, because that would hinder their success. Regardless of where you are on the pathway to success, make sure your thoughts and words are positive. This will help you achieve the success you desire.

6

❦

Establishing Priorities

❧

*Most of us spend too much time on what is urgent
and not enough time on what is important.*

Stephen R. Covey[14]

Stephen R. Covey wrote the popular book *The 7 Habits of Highly Effective People*. I think we all want to be effective and successful, but in order to do this, we must be able to establish priorities. There are four levels of priorities: urgent, high, medium, and low. One way to begin setting your priorities is to list each one, and then put it into the category in which it belongs. This way, you will be able to clearly see them.

A priority is something that is more important than other things that may also be important. We all have priorities, but some people don't know which ones to put first, second, third, and so on. We have already established that if we want to have a success-ful life, God must be our first priority. For me, this is not something I have to think about; it is an ingrained habit. The first thing I do after getting up and mak-ing my coffee each morning is go to the place where I spend my time with God. You may need to arrange your life differently than I do, but however you order your day, God must be a priority.

A priority is something more important than other things that are also important.

There are many opinions on what people's priorities should be, but I will tell you mine. God is first, followed by my family, then taking care of myself, and then my ministry. Besides those four, other situations regularly arise and need my attention. As they come up, I also prioritize them appropriately. In my ministry, my first priority is prayer and then Bible study. After these, I prioritize doing television, preparing for conferences, and writing books.

DON'T PROCRASTINATE

I highly recommend not leaving important things until the last minute. If you do, you will almost surely end up stressed. I always stay ahead on writing my books and preparing the messages I teach. I look at my calendar and see what is coming up over the next several weeks so I can schedule time to complete each task, usually two weeks in advance. This enables me to feel relaxed when the time draws near to actually do what I have prepared to do. When writing books, I stay six months to one year ahead of schedule because books are such big projects. This gives me plenty of time to go over them and make any changes I think will make them better.

I have read in many places that procrastination is a significant stressor. When we know we have to do things and keep putting them off, they weigh heavier on us each day we delay. I advise people to get their hard jobs done first. If there is something you dread doing, just do it and get it over with.

Get your hard jobs done first.

What do you need to change in your life? If you have been doing something wrong, it's never too late to do it right. Don't waste time feeling guilty about the time you already wasted, either. That will only cause you to waste even more time.

I had the wrong priorities for a long time before I realized the error of my ways. For many years, I put my ministry first. It is interesting to note that during those years, the progress toward achieving my goals was very slow. If I could go back and talk to my thirty-five-year-old self, I would tell her that career success should never be a person's top priority. Back then, I thought many things were important, and I now know they are not nearly as important as other things. In fact, some are not important at all. I'll share just two of them with you.

Career success should never be your first priority.

First, I would tell my thirty-five-year-old self that caring too much about what people think of you is a big mistake. If what people think of you is a priority for you, it shouldn't be. Other people's thoughts can't hurt you, and those people aren't thinking about you as much as you imagine they are. When we start making our decisions based on what we think other people want us to do, we are on a slippery slope that will not lead us to a good place. The Greek philosopher Aristotle said, "There is only one way to avoid criticism: do nothing, say nothing, and be nothing."

The only way to avoid criticism is to do nothing, say nothing, and be nothing.

I don't even want to think about how much time I've wasted worrying about what other people think or say about me. Many times in the past, I let other people's urgent problems, needs, and desires take priority over my ministry responsibilities. I ended up feeling rushed, not getting enough sleep, and sometimes trading "excellent" for "good" simply to get a job done. It wasn't until I was about fifty years old that I finally removed the worry about other people's opinions from my priority list. Not knowing how to say no adversely affected my health, and although it took a few years to turn the situation around, I think I can now say "I follow the Holy Spirit, not people."

*Eliminate useless priorities by questioning
your motives for doing them.*

I would also tell my thirty-five-year-old self to have pure motives in all things. Nothing helps us eliminate useless priorities like honestly asking ourselves our true motive for doing them. We only get rewarded from God for what we do with pure motives. I had a situation today that I handled differently than I would have when I was thirty-five. I was asked to speak at an event and said yes. Later, the organizers called and asked me to arrive a day early and do some other things. In my heart, I really didn't want to do that, because going a day early would have meant an overnight stay instead of simply being able to fly in and out on a Saturday. Because the timing wasn't good for me, and because staying overnight required packing, unpacking, and dealing with more travel-related details, I thought through the situation and decided to say no. At thirty-five, I would not have wanted to go a day early but would have felt I "should." I would have feared hurting the hosts' feelings. But I've learned that if I am going to do what God has assigned me to do and stay healthy, then when He says no, I must say no also. I'm a lot older than thirty-five now, and I have learned a lot.

THE IMPORTANCE OF FAMILY

Family is second on my list of priorities. We can look at the way the world is going and plainly see that family is not a high priority for many people today. Dave and I spend time together every day. In addition, I regularly spend time with my children and grandchildren, and I either see or talk to three of my four children every day. One of them lives out of town, and I talk to him several times a week and see him at least once a month.

If you have children, they want your time more than your money. Yes, our children want us to give them money, but if we give them money and things to try to compensate for not spending time with them, we will pay the penalty later in life when we have no relationship with them.

I know a pastor who not only pastored a church but also traveled frequently in the US and abroad when he was younger. He told me that despite his busy schedule, he never missed a ball game in which his two sons were playing. Now he has a phenomenal relationship with his sons, and they both pastor amazing churches. He said there were times when he had to fly all night to get home for one of their games, but he always wanted them to know that they were more important to him than his ministry. If you could hear me right now, you would hear me clapping and congratulating him.

I could have done a better job as a parent than I did when my children were younger. Thankfully, I turned things around in time, and now Dave and I have good relationships with all four of our grown children.

Dave and I have invested much time and effort to keep our marriage strong, and I am proud to say we have been married fifty-seven years, as of the writing of this book. No good relationship stays good by accident. We must be intentional about keeping or making our relationships strong. Relationships involve spending time together and sharing with one another, among other things.

No good relationship stays good by accident.

You can be friendly with everyone, but you can't be great friends with everyone. I read that human beings are only capable of five really good friendships at one time.[15] Pick the five people you really want in your life, and be prepared to invest in them. We should love everyone, but we cannot give everyone enough of our time to call them a "best friend."

If you don't make an effort to have good relationships now, when you get older and have achieved the career success that is so important to you, you may find yourself lonely. A career can't give you a hug when you need one; it cannot comfort you when you are sad; it can't even smile at you. A successful career is God's will for many people, unless it means losing everything else that is really important.

A career can't give you a hug when you need it.

Many so-called successful people have died by suicide, seemingly because their remarkable achievements gave them no joy. I think of Ernest Hemingway, Robin Williams, and Anthony Bourdain, just to mention a few you are probably familiar with. Some of them suffered with depression, which contributed to their death. Vincent van Gogh died by suicide and didn't realize that he would later be regarded as one of the greatest artists in history.

Some people don't realize how important or talented they are because they listen to the lies of the devil. They convince themselves they are worth nothing, and they conclude that without value and purpose they have no reason to live.

TAKING CARE OF YOURSELF

I make myself the third priority on my list, and let me say loud and clear that this is not wrong or selfish. If you don't take care of yourself, eventually you won't have anything to give to anyone else. I worked too hard during the early years when my ministry was growing rapidly, and eventually I paid for it with my health. I wish I had had a mentor to tell me what I am sharing with you now, but most of the people I knew in ministry lived the same way I did. They were working, working, working, and complaining about all the work. Yes, we will have to work hard to be successful, but we also need to live balanced lives.

If you don't take care of yourself, you won't have anything to give to others.

I remember hosting a guest speaker at our church when I was still dreaming of success. He said, "I haven't taken a day off in twelve years." I remember thinking, *He must be very spiritual.* Now I know he was not using wisdom in regard to his health. We do have to work hard, but we will have better overall health if we balance hard work with proper periods of worship, rest, and play.

One way I take care of myself is by doing workouts with a trainer three days a week. He comes to my home, so that keeps me from having to take time to drive to the gym. You may not be able to do that, but you can do something to get some exercise. Another way I care for myself is to get stretched twice each month, which means I see an exercise professional who knows how to stretch people's muscles to help them stay flexible and strong. As I get older, this keeps me flexible. I also get eight hours of sleep about 90 percent of the time. When I don't, it's because I am traveling and doing conferences. In addition, I try to eat healthy meals. Although I do enjoy a dessert occasionally, I don't eat a lot of sugar. I also drink plenty of water, because staying hydrated is extremely important to good health.

I also take care of my skin, teeth, and hair. Since I am on television, it is especially important for me to set a good example. Finally, I work activities I enjoy into my schedule, such as reading a good fiction book, watching a good movie, taking an occasional shopping trip, and playing a card game called Phase 10 with our daughter and son-in-law.

Taking care of yourself when you are young pays off when you are older. Dave has worked out with weights every other day for about sixty-five years, and he looks amazing. He still wears the same size clothes he wore when we married. He feels good and has plenty of energy. Dave has always taken time to rest, have fun, exercise, drink plenty of water, and get a good night's sleep. These are all simple things to do, but many people don't do them.

In the midst of working hard to reach your goals in life, it's important to do things you enjoy. They don't have to be expensive or time consuming. A cup of coffee with a friend or a walk around the neighborhood can be enjoyable and refreshing.

YOUR SUCCESS

I want to say again that to be successful, you must know what your priorities are. Paul teaches us to set our minds and "keep them set" (Colossians 3:2 AMPC). He wrote these words in the context of thinking about the things of heaven instead of the things of earth, but they are good words to remember in the context of priorities too. We need to determine what our priorities are and keep our minds set on them. What are your priorities for your life? What do you want to accomplish with the time, gifts, and talents God has given you? In order to reach your main goal, you must be able to prioritize your days too. For instance, what is most important for you to focus on today? Keep in mind that your priorities may change from day to day based on your short-term and long-term goals. You may need to get one thing done today and something else done tomorrow.

A successful person will be able to choose what needs to be done now and what can wait until later. You won't be successful at setting priorities if you don't take time to do this. If you ask me what I am going to do for the next week, I can tell you because I have a plan. But many people don't even know at two in the afternoon what they will do later that day.

When it comes to determining how you should schedule your time, don't major in the minor things. Another way of saying this is to keep the main thing, the main thing. Perfectionists and extremely detailed people sometimes have a problem with this. They can easily get caught up doing something that isn't important at the expense of something that is.

Perfectionists may often be late for appointments or commitments because they want their house to look perfect when they leave. Or they may spend too much time trying to fix a minor flaw that nobody else would even notice. They then end up pressuring themselves and those who are depending on them. They may even ruin someone else's schedule because they don't know how to prioritize their own. The bottom line is that no one is perfect at everything, and if you try to be great at everything, you will likely end up being good at nothing.

The Holy Spirit will help you prioritize each day if you will listen to His leading. Sometimes it's only a whisper or a knowing in your heart, but He will lead if you will follow. He is the ultimate Helper to teach you how to set your priorities and stick with them.

The Holy Spirit will help you prioritize your life if you will listen.

7

Learn to Be Faithful

Success in God's eyes is faithfulness to His calling.

Billy Graham[16]

The Book of Proverbs teaches us about prudence, meaning good management of our resources. How many people do you suppose never succeed because they won't wisely manage what they have? For example, people won't prosper financially if they immediately spend all the money they earn without saving for the future or for things they want to buy without paying interest. The same goes for their time and their thoughts and words. If they can't manage these well, they most likely won't succeed.

If you want to know what it takes to be a success, read and study Proverbs and follow its principles. A good resource for this is my book *In Search of Wisdom: Life-Changing Truths in the Book of Proverbs*. It guides you, chapter by chapter, through the incredible wisdom found in Proverbs.

God gives us resources according to our ability to handle them.

God gives each of us resources according to our ability to handle them, and He watches to see how we will manage them. Our "promotions" in life are based on how well we do. I liken this to going through school. We go through one grade and learn what is taught, but we need to pass tests before we are promoted to the next grade. People go through this process from kindergarten through high school, college, and beyond. Similarly, in work settings, people receive promotions because they prove themselves knowledgeable and faithful in their current positions and demonstrate the ability to handle greater responsibility.

When I was growing up, the world was much different than it is today. People expected to work hard to deserve what they earned or received. Today many people think they are entitled to things without having to exert effort to earn or deserve them.

The parable of the bags of gold given to three servants is a great example of this:

Again, it will be like a man going on a journey, who called his servants and entrusted his wealth to them. To one he gave five bags of gold, to another two bags, and to another one bag, each according to his ability. Then he went on his journey. The man who had received five bags of gold went at once and put his money to work and gained five bags more. So also, the one with two bags of gold gained two more. But the man who had received one bag went off, dug a hole in the ground and hid his master's money. After a long time the master of those servants returned and settled accounts with them. The man who had received five bags of gold brought the other five. "Master," he said, "you entrusted me with five bags of gold. See, I have gained five more." His master replied, "Well done, good and faithful servant! You have been faithful with a few things; I will put you in charge of many things. Come and share your master's happiness!" The man with two bags of gold also came. "Master," he said, "you entrusted me with two bags of gold; see, I have gained two more." His master replied, "Well done, good and faithful servant! You have been faithful with a few things; I will put you in charge of many things. Come and share your master's happiness!" Then the man who had received one bag of gold came. "Master," he said,

"I knew that you are a hard man, harvesting where you have not sown and gathering where you have not scattered seed. So I was afraid and went out and hid your gold in the ground. See, here is what belongs to you." His master replied, "You wicked, lazy servant! So you knew that I harvest where I have not sown and gather where I have not scattered seed? Well then, you should have put my money on deposit with the bankers, so that when I returned I would have received it back with interest. So take the bag of gold from him and give it to the one who has ten bags. For whoever has will be given more, and they will have an abundance. Whoever does not have, even what they have will be taken from them. And throw that worthless servant outside, into the darkness, where there will be weeping and gnashing of teeth."

Matthew 25:14–30

This is one of the best parables in the Bible about how to succeed. As you take what God gives you and do the most you can with it, you prepare for promotion to the next level. God starts us with small things, such as the first Bible study I taught. Then He watches to see if we will be faithful with it, work hard to make it a success, and obey His instructions along the way. If we do well with the seemingly small things, the next thing will be bigger.

I can see this pattern clearly by looking back at the progress of my ministry. As you read in chapter 2, I started with a home Bible study. First, I taught a Bible study of twelve people, then the group grew to between twenty and twenty-five people each Tuesday evening. I did that for two years before I was asked to do a second Bible study on Thursday afternoons. For me, teaching two Bible studies instead of one was a promotion. During those years I was paid no salary, and no offerings were received for me; I learned to depend on God for literally everything our family needed. Those years also proved that my motive for teaching was not to make money but to serve God.

I only stopped teaching the weekly Bible studies when I felt led to do so. I was sure the next opportunity would be big and come fast. But for an entire year I did *nothing* in ministry—well, nothing except hold on to the dream God had given me. Looking back, I realize that God was doing a lot *in* me, but not *through* me. Often, we must be *prepared* for the next level before we can be *promoted* to it. One of the primary lessons God taught me during that year was to be myself and not feel I had to do everything the way others did. It was a hard year for me, and I found it difficult to not give up on my dream of teaching the Bible all over the world. I wondered if I had made a mistake in stopping the weekly Bible studies. I often felt discouraged, but I could not give up. In my heart, I kept believing that God would open the right door for me at the right time.

> *You must be* prepared *before you can be* promoted.

After that year, the leaders at my church invited me to teach a weekly Bible study for women, and I did that for five years. I almost declined the opportunity because I never felt I was called to teach women exclusively. But since I wasn't doing anything else, I thought it was best to take the offer in front of me.

The first week of that Bible study, 110 women showed up. Our church only had about fifty people, so where did they come from? I can only assume that God got the word out because it was time for my next promotion. I taught that weekly meeting for five years. In the meantime, I was ordained into ministry, invited to join the church staff as an associate pastor, taught in the church's Bible college three times a week, and did a lot of the preaching when the pastor traveled. All this was a *big* promotion for me. At the end of five years, about 450 women were attending the weekly meeting, and I was on a fifteen-minute radio program. That five-year season was a time of much growth and many opportunities for me, all serving as preparation for the next place God wanted to take me.

You may feel dormant or overlooked for a long time. You may wonder if your dream will ever come true. Then suddenly, if you have been faithful and when He has prepared you, God will move and do amazing things.

FROM GOOD TO BETTER

Even though God had promoted me in remarkable ways at the church, after about five years teaching the women's Bible study, serving as an associate pastor, teaching in the Bible college, and fulfilling other roles at the church, I began to feel restless in my soul. The feeling did not go away, so I began seriously searching for what was wrong.

God made clear to me that He wanted me to take the ministry north, south, east, and west. I waited one year before obeying Him, and during that time I grew more and more miserable.

Eventually my pastor asked me what was wrong. Out of my mouth came "I don't know, but maybe I shouldn't be here anymore." He had a surprised look on his face, and I am sure I did too because I had never even considered leaving. He said, "Well, you better take some time off and find out."

I started a fast, intending to continue it, along with prayer, until I received a clear answer from God concerning my job at the church. But it only took about one hour, and I knew I had to leave my position. My priorities were changing quickly.

You may wonder how I knew what to do. First, I felt very definite and settled in my heart that leaving was what God wanted. Dave had been telling me for quite a while that I needed to leave my job and stretch out my borders. I also had several strong confirmations from other people who knew nothing of what was in my heart. Without any direct knowledge of my situation, one woman asked, "How long do you think you will stay here?" Another said, "You won't be here forever because God wants to use you to help more people."

The decision to leave my job at the church was one of the most difficult choices I have ever made. I loved my job, I loved the people, and I enjoyed what I was doing. But God spoke definitively and let me know He didn't need me there anymore.

Frankly, I struggled to keep from feeling insulted, because I had been at the church from the time it only had thirty people. I had seen it grow to about 1,500, and we had just moved into a new building. I felt I had been there for all the hard work and would miss the great days ahead. What I was doing was good, but God had something better in mind. Had I not obeyed Him, I would still be there, but I would be dissatisfied because that wasn't where He needed me. I would also have missed all the amazing things God has allowed me to do over the thirty-seven years since I left that job.

If we are going to follow God, we may not get to do everything we want to do. In other words, we may have to give up what we think we want so God can give us what we really want, but we just don't know it yet.

If you follow God, you may not get to do everything you want to do.

After I left my position at the church, Joyce Meyer Ministries was born. Dave and I finished the basement of our home and put our offices there. We set out like Abraham did, not knowing where we were headed (Hebrews 11:8). We simply tried to follow the guidance of the Holy Spirit, and we still do that today.

We contracted with eight radio stations, and our programs did fairly well. We held local meetings in the St. Louis area. We held meetings once a month in north St. Louis, and we had weekly meetings in areas in the south, east, and west of the city. I had to stay around St. Louis because no one knew me in other cities. But I did exactly what God said to do: I went north, south, east, and west.

We had a handful of employees who helped us greatly, and Dave and I worked very hard. I remember sitting in my office, answering the few pieces of mail we received using my manual typewriter. As the radio audience grew, we started renting hotel ballrooms where we could hold conferences of one hundred to two hundred people. We had to hold the meetings within driving distance of our home near St. Louis, Missouri, because we certainly could not afford plane tickets. Dave located and rented the ballrooms and continued working diligently to get me on more radio stations. Eventually, God directed us to go on television weekly and then daily. As we showed ourselves faithful in each thing God gave us to do, after a while,

He gave us more. Being faithful over little things is the key to eventually having something big to be faithful over (Matthew 25:23). Your situation probably is not the same as mine was, but the same godly principles apply no matter what your goals are.

FAITHFUL AND PATIENT

After we went on television, the conferences we hosted grew much larger, and I began receiving invitations to speak at other events or various churches. Before long, I couldn't keep up with all the promotions God was sending into my life. He says that He will open the windows of heaven and pour out so many blessings that we won't be able to contain them (Malachi 3:10), and I think that's what happened in our ministry.

Eventually, I had to start choosing which speaking invitations to say yes to and which to say no to simply because I couldn't do everything people asked. But please remember, this didn't happen overnight. I started by teaching a small Bible study once a week.

The success I later experienced didn't come easily or quickly.

We receive God's promises through faith and patience (Hebrews 6:12). Patience is not only the ability to wait. It has a lot to do with our attitude and how we behave while we wait. Everyone waits, whether they want to or not. We can make ourselves miserable while we wait, or we can learn to wait well. If you are in a waiting period right now, keep a good attitude and trust that God will bring promotion and breakthrough at just the right time.

You can make yourself miserable while you wait, or you can learn to wait well.

There is nothing we can do to make God hurry. As a matter of fact, if we get too impatient, we usually end up taking matters into our own hands and doing something to move things along faster. This usually doesn't turn out well, and we end up waiting longer than we would have waited had we continued to trust God.

Everything in the ministry grew *very slowly*. I wanted it to grow faster, but Dave was—and is—an extremely patient man. Part of being faithful is being patient. Dave knew that if we became successful too fast, it would produce pride in us, and the ministry would fail. If it happened slowly, we would have to deal with a variety of issues, tests, and situations that would work humility in us, along with the conviction that we could not do it without God. If you want to do something that is a success God's way, you will need to learn to wait with a good attitude. Trust that God's timing is perfect and that His way is always best.

As our ministry grew little by little, I learned so many lessons, many of them painful. But I now say the wait was extremely valuable. I wanted to give up numerous times during the years of preparation, but I am glad now that God gave me the grace to hold on.

Whatever your dream is, be faithful to do what God leads you to do. As you remain faithful, and as you are patient while the process unfolds, you will experience the success God desires for you to enjoy. If I can give one piece of advice, I would say be sure to enjoy where you are on the way to where you are going. Don't focus so intensely on getting to your destination that you don't take time to enjoy your journey.

Don't focus so intensely on your destination that you don't enjoy your journey.

8

The Necessity of Discipline and Self-Control

The dictionary is the only place that success comes before work. Work is the key to success, and hard work can help you accomplish anything.

Vince Lombardi Jr.[17]

I hope you don't decide to skip this chapter because discipline and self-control don't sound exciting to you. I don't believe people can ever be successful without these two qualities. Ecclesiastes 5:3 says that "a dream comes with much business and painful effort" (AMPC). Having a dream or desire to be successful is easy, but if people are not willing to work hard, often for a long time, they won't succeed. Margaret Thatcher said, "I don't know anyone who has got to the top without hard work."[18]

You must be able to manage yourself before you can manage others.

The reason I think discipline and self-control are vital to success is that you must be able to manage yourself before you can manage anything or anyone else. When you reach the top, you no longer have a boss, so you must be able to manage yourself. This includes managing your attitudes, the way you treat people, your thoughts and words, how you spend or don't spend money, how you take care of yourself, and many other things.

Even if you are the boss, accountability is important. This could mean being accountable to a mentor, a consultant, or a board. In fact, many businesses and ministries—large and small—have a board of people who help oversee their activities and weigh in on the decisions the boss is considering.

On a daily basis, God is my only boss. But I also have my husband and four grown children plus a board who would all confront me if they felt I was doing something I should not do.

It is easy to be deceived, especially where money and power are concerned, so use wisdom and ask a few good people with integrity and experience to correct you if they think you are going in the wrong direction.

Sadly, I can think of several successful people who lost their ministries or businesses due to dishonesty, sexual immorality, mistreating people, or various addictions. One man, when asked why he did what he did, said, "I had so much power I thought I could do anything I wanted to do, and nobody would dare question me." I can also think of some people who failed simply because they were too prideful to listen to anyone else. Sometimes, others can see in us what we don't see ourselves. If two or three spiritually mature people tell you the same thing, it is wise to listen.

Self-control is the ability to say no to yourself, no matter how much you want to do something, if you know it is the wrong thing to do.

Self-control is the ability to say no to yourself.

Proverbs 6:6–11 tells us to study the ant and notice how it works hard without an overseer. The little ant has the wisdom to do what is right without being forced to. I am working right now, but I don't have to. I could have done anything I wanted to do today, but I have responsibilities to fulfill, and I want to be faithful to do the best I can for God.

Almost every morning when I get up, I can choose to do whatever I want that day, but if I didn't choose to work most days, I wouldn't be where I am today. As I mentioned earlier, procrastination derails a lot of people who have the ability to do great things. They keep putting off the work their dream will require until another time. Somehow that time never comes. Someone rightly said, "Someday is not a day of the week." If you are going to put off anything, put off procrastinating.

GO THE EXTRA MILE

Successful people not only are willing to work hard; they often go the extra mile. They are wise to do a little more than is required or make extra provisions, because situations often demand more than they think. Jesus' parable of the ten virgins is a great example of this:

> Then the kingdom of heaven shall be likened to ten virgins who took their lamps and went to meet the bridegroom. Five of them were foolish (thoughtless, without forethought) and five were wise (sensible, intelligent, and prudent). For when the foolish took their lamps, they did not take any [extra] oil with them; but the wise took flasks of oil along with them [also] with their lamps. While the bridegroom lingered and

was slow in coming, they all began nodding their heads, and they fell asleep. But at midnight there was a shout, Behold, the bridegroom! Go out to meet him! Then all those virgins got up and put their own lamps in order. And the foolish said to the wise, Give us some of your oil, for our lamps are going out. But the wise replied, There will not be enough for us and for you; go instead to the dealers and buy for yourselves. But while they were going away to buy, the bridegroom came, and those who were prepared went in with him to the marriage feast; and the door was shut.

Matthew 25:1–10 AMPC

We can learn many great lessons from this parable. The first is that we should do more than we think we need to. The five foolish virgins were not properly prepared. They only did the bare minimum. They did not make provision for their lamps in case the bridegroom was late. And then, for some reason, he was.

In many situations, too much is better than too little. This could relate to preparing for a project or opportunity, allowing extra time to get to an important appointment, or saving more money for a certain purchase or project than you expect to spend. It could mean not starting a road trip and thinking you'll fill your gas tank fifty miles down the road. Start with a full tank because you never know when you could run into a traffic jam or some other delay. Develop the wisdom to know that circumstances don't always unfold as you expect, and discipline yourself to do what you need to if they don't—and a little bit more.

The second lesson is that, in many situations, we will deal with people who don't do what they should—like the five foolish virgins who didn't have enough oil. When this happens, they typically want people who have been wise and disciplined, thought ahead, and prepared for the unexpected to rescue them, like the foolish virgins did with the wise. They want those who have worked hard to give them what they should have earned for themselves.

The third lesson this parable teaches us is that success does not happen because we wish for it. Wanting it is not enough. The bridegroom arrived while the foolish virgins were out shopping for more oil. The five wise virgins set good boundaries. They did not share their oil with the foolish ones, but allowed them to learn from their mistakes. I am sure that when the foolish virgins returned, they wished they had taken extra oil with them. Many people wish for success, but we can't wish our way to achieving it. Success comes because we discipline ourselves to prepare for it and work for it.

Success does not happen by wishing for it.

DON'T BE RUDE

Because it is considered rude to walk into a church service during the worship music and disturb those who are trying to worship God while squeezing past them to get a seat, I know of a few churches who close the doors to the sanctuary when the music begins. Those who are late arriving to the service have to wait until the music concludes before they can enter the room. Because they were late, the doors were shut. This reminds me of what happened to the five foolish virgins. They were late, and the door was shut to them.

Some churches allow late arrivals to stand in the back of the sanctuary until the worship music is over, but they won't allow them to disturb other people. I believe this is the right way to handle the situation.

Anyone can be late occasionally, sometimes for good or unavoidable reasons, but some people make a habit of being late. These people do not show love and respect to others, because they interrupt them while they are doing something important. Being on time takes discipline, and if you struggle to discipline yourself, becoming more punctual is a good and fairly easy place to start practicing discipline.

Some churchgoers also have a bad habit of walking out while the pastor is giving an invitation for people to surrender their lives to Jesus. How sad it would be if someone were hindered from accepting Christ as their Lord and Savior because a fellow Christian distracted them—just to get out of the parking lot ahead of everyone else. Hurrying is a huge problem today, and those who procrastinate are the ones who hurry the most.

I recently read a book called *The Ruthless Elimination of Hurry* by John Mark Comer. He makes the great observation that we cannot love people if we are always in a hurry. Love is the number one call of God on our lives as believers. The Bible teaches that loving others is the most important thing we do (1 Peter 4:8), and hurrying is the best way to miss those who need our love most. Taking time to be with other people is one way to show them we love them.

ALWAYS DO YOUR BEST

If you don't go the extra mile, as Matthew 5:41 teaches, you may reap what you have sown (Galatians 6:7), as we read in the story about the carpenter below. I think this story illustrates the importance of disciplining ourselves to do our best at all times. We should never slack off when it comes to our integrity or work ethic, even if we are tired and ready to move on to something else. We should always discipline ourselves to finish well.

Always go the extra mile, because you reap what you sow.

An elderly carpenter was ready to retire. He told his employer of his plans to leave the house-building business and live a more leisurely life with his wife and enjoy his extended family. He would miss the paycheck, but the time was right and he was ready to hang up his hammer.

His boss was disappointed, as the carpenter had been a loyal and diligent worker for many years, so he was sad to see him go.

He asked for one last favor, requesting that the carpenter build just one more house before retiring. The carpenter said yes, but in time it was easy to see that his heart was not in his work. He resorted to shoddy workmanship and used inferior materials. It was an unfortunate way to end a dedicated career.

When the carpenter finished his work, his boss came to inspect the house. He handed the front door key to the carpenter. "This is your house," he said, "my gift to you." The carpenter was shocked! What a shame! If he had only known he was building his own house, he would have done it all so differently. Now he had to live in the home he had built none too well.

DISCIPLINED PEOPLE KNOW HOW TO SAY NO

Disciplined people know how to say no to others. But more important, they know how to say no to themselves. They know they cannot do everything and do anything well. I was recently with our three-and-a-half-year-old grandson, and one of many things he says is "I don't like it when you tell me no!" He is emphatic and loud when he says this. His parents correct him, but it makes me laugh because he is so young to be saying this. It's cute coming from a three-and-a-half-year-old, but when people who are thirty or forty years of age say it, it is no longer cute. We must learn that *no* is part of life and trust that there are times in life when *no* is the best answer.

Hebrews 12:11 (AMPC) says:

For the time being no discipline brings joy, but seems grievous and painful; but afterwards it yields a peaceable fruit of righteousness to those who have been trained by it [a harvest of fruit which consists in righteousness—in conformity to God's will in purpose, thought, and action, resulting in right living and right standing with God].

When you are in the process of disciplining yourself, it does seem "grievous and painful." But if you stick with it, you will eventually be glad you did because it will produce good fruit in your life. Are you able to do now what will benefit you later? Most of us want all the blessings, advantages, success, and prosperity we can have in life, but not everyone wants to do the work to get these things. Many people today want instant gratification, but that is not God's way. Believe me, working and waiting for what we want makes us appreciate it much more than if it is simply handed to us.

Do now what will benefit you later.

I tell people who struggle with jealousy of others not to ever be jealous of what someone else has unless they are willing to do what that person did to get it. We can easily look at what another person has and say, "I wish I had that," but I can guarantee you that they didn't get it by wishing.

God has given us a spirit of discipline and self-control to help us succeed in every aspect of life, and we can choose to use it or not (2 Timothy 1:7). What lies in our power to do also lies in our power to not do. Power must be harnessed and directed to do any good. As Harry Emerson Fosdick said, "No horse gets anywhere until he is harnessed. No stream or gas ever drives anything until it is confined. No Niagara is ever turned into light and power until it is tunneled. No life ever grows great until it is focused, dedicated, disciplined."[19]

Self-discipline is required in order to work hard and also to maintain balance and *not* work too hard. Balance is important in life. First Peter 5:8 in the Amplified Bible, Classic Edition teaches us to be well balanced so we don't give the devil an opportunity to damage or destroy us. Based on this verse, I conclude that the devil doesn't mind if we do too little or too much, because either one can prevent us from being successful.

The devil doesn't mind if you do too little or too much.

You may be a naturally hard worker, as I am. If so, you may need to be more diligent in disciplining yourself to rest than to work. Remember, in addition to getting enough rest, also take time to do things you enjoy to avoid burnout.

FAITH WITHOUT WORKS

We are saved by grace through faith alone (Ephesians 2:8), not because of any work we do. Salvation is a gift that opens the door to all the other blessings of God, but they come with conditions, such as obedience to God, hard work, loving others, prayer, faithfulness, diligence, forgiving those who have hurt you, and others. To use a metaphor, Jesus has opened the prison doors of living in bondage to sin, but we have to walk out of the prison. I have heard stories about people who spent many years in prison, and when they were finally released because they had served their sentences, they immediately committed another crime so they would be put back in prison. They didn't know how to live in freedom and make their own decisions and choices.

The story of the elephant who was free but didn't know it illustrates my point well:

As a man was passing some elephants, he suddenly stopped, confused by the fact that these huge creatures were being held by only a small rope tied to their front leg. No chains, no cages. It was obvious that the elephants could, at any time, break away from their bonds, but for some reason, they did not.

He saw a trainer nearby and asked why these animals just stood there and made no attempt to get away. "Well," the trainer said, "when they were very young, and much smaller, we used the same size rope to tie them. At that age, it's enough to hold them. As they grow up, they are conditioned to believe they cannot break away. They believe the rope can still hold them, so they never try to break free."

The man was amazed. These elephants could at any time break free from their bonds, but because they believed they couldn't, they were stuck right where they were.

Be sure you are not living less than an abundant life because you have been conditioned to believe that is all you can have. God created the blessings He wants us to have, but we must walk in them. Ephesians 2:10 says we are God's workmanship, "created in Christ Jesus for good works, which God prepared beforehand that we should walk in them" (NKJV). You can experience every blessing and success He has for you, but you'll need discipline and self-control to walk in them.

Do not live a less than abundant life because you have been conditioned to do so.

9

The Easy Way

The first and best victory is to conquer self.
To be conquered by self is, of all things,
the most shameful and objectionable.

Plato[20]

People who do not practice discipline and self-control often look for the easy way to do things. I urge you *not* to do this. You may ask, "Joyce, are you serious? Why would I not take the easy way if it's available?"

Had Jesus taken the easy way, this book could not have been written. Because true success God's way wouldn't even be available to us.

Moses grew up as the son of Pharaoh's daughter, with all the privileges and advantages afforded a ruler's family (Exodus 2:1–10). But he knew he was an Israelite. The time came when he refused to be called the son of Pharaoh's daughter any longer because he preferred to be mistreated with the people of God rather than enjoy the fleeting pleasures of sin (Hebrews 11:24–25). Had he not made this decision, he would not have been positioned to lead the Israelites out of slavery in Egypt, to experience the parting of the Red Sea, or to climb Mount Sinai to receive the Ten Commandments from God.

I wonder how many blessings people miss because they choose to do something the easy way. Let's not do that. It is far better to do what is hard and live a blessed life than to take the easy way out and live an unhappy one.

What are some ways you can practice not taking
the easy way in your everyday life? Here are some
ideas:

- Take the stairs instead of the elevator or
  escalator (unless you are going to the
  twentieth floor).
- Finish your work before you entertain
  yourself.
- Skip dessert if you need to lose a few pounds.
- Don't put off dealing with unpleasant
  situations.
- When you have several jobs to do, do the one
  you most dislike first.
- Never put off until tomorrow what can and
  should be done today.
- Don't use credit to pay for anything you don't
  have to have.
- Always save some of the money you make.
- Take time to be kind to everyone.
- Get some kind of exercise at least three or four
  times a week.
- Slow down (this is difficult for busy people).

- Practice patience, and wait with a good attitude.
- Be very generous.

These things, and others like them, will help you gain the success that you want, but they will require discipline and self-control. "Self" (human nature without God's love and grace) often chooses the easy path in life, but it leads us to the "lower life." We read about this in the Amplified Bible, Classic Edition rendering of Matthew 10:39: "Whoever finds his [lower] life will lose it [the higher life], and whoever loses his [lower] life on My account will find it [the higher life]." In other words, if we do what is not easy, we will find the higher life— the successful life Jesus desires for us. But if we pursue the easy, lower life, we will lose the higher life.

The easy path in life leads to a lower life.

We will not be successful without discipline, self-control, and, in most cases, other people to help us.

Practicing discipline and self-control by making sure we treat them well is an important key to success. I am greatly saddened when I see a leader (someone with authority or power) mistreating their coworkers simply because they can.

I've heard disturbing stories about how some very wealthy people behave in restaurants and other places of business, and it doesn't sound like they practice any self-control at all. Don't ever let financial blessings make you think you are better than others. Use money to be a blessing to people. Support the preaching of the gospel, help the poor, meet needs wherever you find them, and thank God that He has equipped you with the ability to experience the joy of being a blessing. As Acts 20:35 says, "It is more blessed to give than to receive."

WHAT DOES THE APOSTLE PAUL SAY ABOUT DISCIPLINE AND SELF-CONTROL?

Paul understood the value of not taking the easy way. He knew he had to exercise discipline and self-control to properly teach others. To teach, lead, or be a parent, knowing that your students or children will follow your example, is both a privilege and responsibility. For this reason, it is vital for me to set a good example at home and everywhere I go. This requires self-control, which I don't always exercise as I should. But I have come a long way from where I began, and I keep growing. One thing that is extremely important to me is treating people the way Jesus would treat them, and it's not always easy.

Paul writes in 1 Corinthians 9:25–27 (ESV):

Every athlete exercises self-control in all things. They do it to receive a perishable wreath, but we an imperishable. So I do not run aimlessly; I do not box as one beating the air. But I discipline my body and keep it under control, lest after preaching to others I myself should be disqualified.

Paul didn't allow himself to do whatever he felt like doing. He practiced self-control and disciplined himself to do what he believed Jesus would have him do.

Paul said yes to God and no to himself to remain qualified to preach to others. He would have been a hypocrite had he told others what to do and then not done it himself. No one likes or trusts a hypocrite. Even Jesus spoke strong words about hypocrisy and issued a scathing rebuke to the hypocrites around Him in Matthew 23. Ask yourself if you are being a good example to other people or merely telling them what they should do. Talk is easy; it costs you nothing, but right action is often costly or requires us to sacrifice in some way.

Talk is easy, and it costs you nothing.

Paul also writes, "All things are lawful for me, but all things are not helpful. All things are lawful for me, but I will not be brought under the power of any" (1 Corinthians 6:12 NKJV). This tells us that Paul knew he was free from the law. He wouldn't lose his salvation if he didn't use self-control, but he also knew that failing to control himself would not help him live in victory or succeed at what God had called him to do. He decided not to allow anything on earth to dominate him. We can do a lot of things and still go to heaven, but undisciplined people will enjoy their lives more if they begin to practice discipline and use self-control.

I can abuse and mistreat my physical body by eating junk food all the time, not getting enough rest, never exercising, and making other unhealthy decisions and still go to heaven. But I will also feel bad physically, deplete my energy reserves, and eventually get sick. I'll go to heaven, but I won't be happy while I am here on earth.

You can worry all the time and go to heaven, but you'll have no peace on earth.

Similarly, we can worry all the time and go to heaven, but we will be anxious and without peace while on earth. People who have received Jesus as Lord and Savior can disrespect and mistreat people and still go to heaven, but they will also lose the respect of others and the opportunity to enjoy good relationships while on earth.

Paul notes in 1 Corinthians 6:13 that without self-control, sexual immorality can become a problem. I can't think of many areas of life that don't require self-control: our thoughts, our words, our attitudes, our finances, our work ethic, our treatment of other people, caring for ourselves, keeping God first in our life, taking care of the things God blesses us with, and maintaining good relationships, to name a few. Self-control is a fruit of the Holy Spirit, which God has given us (Galatians 5:22–23), and it is our friend. Without it we will get into trouble.

Paul met a man named Felix who heard him speaking about faith in Christ (Acts 24:24). Acts 24:25 says, "As Paul talked about righteousness, self-control and the judgment to come, Felix was afraid and said, 'That's enough for now! You may leave. When I find it convenient, I will send for you.'" Like most people, Felix would have preferred to hear what I call a "dessert" message—something that just made him feel good and didn't require any sacrifice on his part. Perhaps he would have continued listening had Paul preached about God's blessings and how wonderful it would be to go to heaven. However, Felix became alarmed when Paul started talking about self-control. Perhaps he thought of how his life would need to change if he had to obey what Paul was saying.

WHAT DOES THE APOSTLE PETER SAY ABOUT DISCIPLINE AND SELF-CONTROL?

Peter taught what Paul taught: *liberty with limits.* We have liberty because Christ has set us free (Galatians 5:1). We no longer live under the law of the Old Covenant. The Bible gives us many instructions and commands, but it also leaves many things to our discretion. God does not control us. He gives us wisdom, but we have to choose to use it. Not using wisdom leads to negative consequences. For instance, I can go into debt and live under constant financial pressure. This won't keep me out of heaven, but it won't give me the successful, victorious life I desire.

I mentioned earlier that our ministry has never borrowed money. We have never been in debt, and this one thing has saved us tremendous stress. Of course, to stay out of debt, we must have the patience to wait for the things we want by saving money for them instead of borrowing. I am not saying that borrowing money is sinful. But anytime you can avoid it, it is wise to do so.

Sometimes people who think they are free feel they can do anything they want, even if it hurts other people. But the love of God that dwells inside us urges us to use self-control. First Peter 2:16–17 teaches us to "Live as people who are free, not using your freedom as a cover-up for evil, but living as servants of God. Honor everyone. Love the brotherhood. Fear God. Honor the emperor" (ESV).

Many people today demand their rights and liberties. But as they do, they often hurt other people. What about a person who demands the right to post pornography on the internet, and it ruins countless marriages or corrupts the minds of young people? Those who post it may claim that posting explicit content is their right of free speech, but would someone who walks in true love do something like that?

Our society is being destroyed through people's selfishness and greed, by those who have no regard for the ways their actions affect other people.

Second Peter 1:3–7 gives us a formula for success if we want to live godly lives:

> His divine power has given us everything we need for a godly life through our knowledge of him who called us by his own glory and goodness. Through these he has given us his very great and precious promises, so that through them you may participate in the divine nature, having escaped the corruption in the world caused by evil desires. For this very reason, make every effort to add to your faith goodness; and to goodness, knowledge; and to knowledge, self-control; and to self-control, perseverance; and to perseverance, godliness; and to godliness, mutual affection; and to mutual affection, love.

God's power makes available to us everything we need for the kind of life He wants us to live. But notice that "for this very reason" we are to "make every effort to add" to our faith goodness, knowledge, self-control, perseverance, godliness, mutual affection, and love. Once again, we see that God does His part, and we need to do ours. I love being in partnership with God. He not only does His part; He also gives us the Holy Spirit to help us do ours.

Our end goal in life should always be love. The kind of love God shows us will lead us to live in ways that bring great success in whatever we do.

WHAT IS REAL FREEDOM?

Real freedom is being free to live in moderation in all things. Moderation brings balance to our lives. We are free to do things, but we have the discipline to keep from doing them in excess.

Real freedom is living in moderation.

It is important to keep in mind that we need to succeed at being people of good character before we can truly succeed in business or other ventures. People of good character live in moderation. They don't look for the easy way; they are able to discipline and control themselves.

Interestingly, Philippians 4:5, in the King James Version of the Bible, is translated "Let your moderation be known unto all men. The Lord is at hand." It seems to me that Paul believes that the Lord's return will happen soon, so we need to make sure we are living in moderation—which of course requires self-control.

Here are a few examples of how we can live in freedom yet exercise self-control:

- We are free to eat candy, but we don't have to eat it every day.
- We are free to express ourselves and say what we think about things but also to keep quiet when we know God is prompting us to.
- We should keep our homes neat and clean but not be so rigid and legalistic that no one can enjoy living there.
- We may enjoy watching television but need to have the self-control not to watch inappropriate content.
- We should enjoy the fruit of our labors but also avoid selfishness and be a blessing to other people.

- If our business is successful and profits increase, we should share them in some way with the employees who helped us get them instead of spending them all on ourselves.

THE BETTER WE TREAT PEOPLE, THE MORE SUCCESSFUL WE WILL BE

I have had the unfortunate experience of working for someone who had little regard for other people. He used them to gain success for himself but never gave them credit for their part in the process. He rarely even said "Thank you." Sadly, people in authority frequently act this way. They use people to gain success instead of using their success to be a blessing to others.

Use your success to be a blessing to others.

At Joyce Meyer Ministries, we don't have a great deal of staff turnover because we treat our employees well. My experience working for someone who did not treat people well taught me a lesson that has helped me in my ministry. I know people need to feel valued if we hope they will continue doing their jobs. Capable people need to be promoted. Their salaries need to allow them to live comfortably, and they value benefits such as insurance, ample vacation time, and a retirement plan. They need to know they are appreciated. I urge you to be sparing with criticism and generous with compliments.

Treat others as you would want to be treated.

Always think of how you would want to be treated, and then treat other people that way. Some businesspeople think, *I can't afford to do the things you are talking about, Joyce.* People may feel that way, but they should consider how expensive it is to lose a trained employee, have to search for another one, and then absorb the cost of training someone else.

At one of the places I do business, the front desk

requires several employees to handle the check-in and checkout processes. The staff there changes constantly. Because of the turnover, I frequently deal with employees who don't know how to work the system properly or answer my questions accurately. As I wait to do my business, I am surrounded by frustrated people having the same experiences I am having. When I ask why there is so much staff turnover, the answer is always "They don't pay people enough here. As soon as they find another job that pays more, they leave." The owners of this business obviously haven't realized how much it costs them to keep losing people, find new employees, and train them. Neither have they considered how much business they lose because people become frustrated trying to get good service.

There is a difference between being frugal and being cheap. When it comes to people, do the most you can for them, not the least you can.

There is a difference between being frugal and being cheap.

Dave and I like to eat at a certain restaurant in St. Louis. The waiters and waitresses have worked there so long that I've heard that people who want to work in this restaurant have to wait for someone to retire before they can get a job there. That in itself tells me the people who own this restaurant treat their staff well. People will not continue to work at a place long if they are being taken advantage of.

Here is one of the best pieces of advice I can offer you if you want to be successful in business: Treat the people who help you succeed with excellence and make them feel important and valued. Doing this requires self-control, because you will have to spend some of the money you may prefer to keep in order to retain them. The truth is that being kind to people doesn't hurt you; it helps you.

It doesn't hurt to be kind to others.

In closing this chapter, let me suggest that you think seriously about what you have read about treating people well. Ask yourself how you are doing in this area. Don't just have a plan to make money; also have a plan to bless the people who help you make that money. This is crucial to success. If business is not your goal, you can still apply this principle to anything you want to do in life, and it will work in your favor.

Let me also suggest that you consider how you think about trying to take the easy way out of things. Hopefully this chapter has helped you understand that the easy way is rarely, if ever, the best way to do things. Be willing to put in the work necessary to achieve your dream, even if it seems hard or if your progress seems slow at times. When you succeed, you'll be glad you did.

10

Excellence and
Integrity

Excellence is the result of habitual integrity.

Lennie Bennett[21]

As Christians, we are called to be excellent. Second Peter 1:3 says, "For His divine power has bestowed upon us all things that [are requisite and suited] to life and godliness, through the [full, personal] knowledge of Him *Who called us by and to His own glory and excellence (virtue)*" (AMPC, emphasis mine). We serve God, who is excellent, and to properly represent Him, we must be excellent also. My concern is that in our modern society many people don't know what excellence is. They have few, if any, examples to learn from.

Because I have lived a long time, I have seen many changes in our society. Although some of them have been positive, many have been negative. When I was a teenager most people were nice. They were well-mannered. They worked hard and did their jobs with excellence, and they kept their word. Quality craftsmanship was something people were proud of. People were honorable and did their duty. They valued integrity. Today, what I have described is not always or even usually the case. Mediocrity has become the norm, and people have become so accustomed to it that they don't see anything wrong with it.

When Dave and I started Joyce Meyer Ministries in

1985, God let me know that if we wanted to be successful, we needed to do three things:

1. Be excellent in all we do.
2. Walk in integrity.
3. Keep strife out of our lives and our ministry.

Since that time, we have been diligent to do these things, and we still teach these principles to our staff on a regular basis. Dave and I also work with God to maintain them in our personal lives.

In 1985, we had very little, but we had an excellent attitude toward what we did have. Our van was old and needed new tires. But we kept it clean, got regular oil changes, and took care of other required maintenance issues. The gatherings we hosted were small, but I studied and preached as though the crowds numbered thousands upon thousands. We only had a few employees, but we paid them the best we could and treated them well. I admit that I made mistakes in how I treated some people in the beginning, especially those I found difficult to get along with. But I have since learned that we are not all alike. We need to make allowances for one another and be rich in mercy toward one another.

If you want to be a success in life, do everything you do with excellence. Excellence is not perfection; it is simply doing the best you can with what you have.

These days, finding people to work with who are excellent and have integrity is difficult, but I am proud to say that Joyce Meyer Ministries has a wonderful staff of people who have been taught excellence. They help enable our ministry to help millions of people around the world.

Do everything you do with excellence.

CHOOSE YOUR FRIENDS CAREFULLY

God's Word teaches us to choose our friends carefully (Proverbs 22:24–25; 1 Corinthians 15:33). This is important if we want to live in excellence and integrity. Our friends influence us greatly, in either positive ways or negative ways.

Find people who are excellent, and spend your time with them. Be sure you are surrounded by people who model what you hope to become. I want friends who walk in love and are not easily angered. I want them to be flexible, emotionally stable, and disciplined. It's important to me that my friends do things on time and keep their word. I would like them to be generous and good to other people and to have good manners. I want friends who talk about meaningful things, but who also listen. In addition, I want them to know how to say "I was wrong," or "I'm sorry," and who are quick to forgive when I say I was wrong or when I apologize. I realize this is a tall order, but I actually do know a few people who fit this description, and I admire them greatly.

EXCELLENCE AND INTEGRITY GO TOGETHER

To have integrity is to be honest in all you do. This kind of honesty represents excellence. To have integrity means to act on one's strong commitment to high moral standards. A person with integrity is authentic, not phony. They live the life they tell others to live, and they do the right thing even when no one is looking. Let me repeat: They do the right thing even when no one is looking. They keep their word and do what they say they will do.

People with integrity do the right thing even when no one is looking.

Some simple, practical examples of integrity are calling someone back when you tell them you'll return their call and keeping your commitments even if you are invited to do something you know you would enjoy more.

When people contact Joyce Meyer Ministries, we respond to them. If they have a question or ask for prayer, we communicate with them. Don't tell someone you will pray for them and then not do it.

When Dave and I have appointments with contractors to do certain jobs in our home, many times they simply don't show up for the appointment or even call to let us know that they are not coming. When we contact them, the excuse is usually "Well, we got busy," or "We're overbooked today," or "The part we needed for the repair didn't come in." But they didn't call to let us know not to expect them. When we make arrangements to be home on a certain day and people don't come to do their job, we waste a portion of our day because they could not be bothered to take the time to make a simple phone call. Actions such as these are rude and lacking in excellence and integrity.

Excellence in communication is vital for anyone who wants to be a success. When we don't communicate, it costs someone else work, time, or money. I am a communicator, and nothing frustrates me more than people who waste my time because they don't bother to communicate. I believe communication is so vital to success that people who don't communicate should probably reconsider whether they should be in business.

EXCELLENCE IN BUSINESS

If you have a business, run it with excellence. Three times at the same restaurant I have ordered a cheeseburger to go, and when I got home it had no cheese.

How do you have a cheeseburger with no cheese? I told someone about this, and they said, "I can top that. I ordered a cheeseburger to go at the same restaurant. When I bit into it, it only had bread, pickles, and ketchup. There was no hamburger or cheese!" Problems such as these cannot be blamed solely on employees. They scream "poor management."

Dave and I frequently go to a local deli. We usually get food to go, but recently we decided to stay there and eat. When I went to the bathroom, the door was lopsided in the frame, and I had to shove it hard to get it closed. I then recalled that the same door had been the same way when I was in that restroom several months earlier. I also noticed that the floor was dirty, and dirt was caked in the corners and along the baseboards. This restaurant does a lot of business, and the food is good, but there is no excuse for not cleaning properly and for not having the door fixed. I wonder if the food I am eating from this place is handled as casually as the cleaning and maintenance. I hope not.

Dave and I often order food to go because of our lifestyle. I can say without hesitation that nearly half the time something is not right about the order. When this happens, it cannot be an accident. It is the result of poor management. But there is one restaurant we order from where I don't think anything has ever been wrong with our meals. This is due to good management. This is the same restaurant where someone has to retire in order for someone else to be hired. Obviously, their spirit of excellence affects all the aspects of their business.

Paying attention to details is important.

When places of business are not kept clean, when orders aren't filled properly, when jobs are consistently done wrong, or when representatives don't keep their commitment, the reason is often that people want to make a lot of profit but are unwilling to put any of their proceeds into keeping the establishment in excellent condition. Eventually businesses like this fail. It may take a while, but when they operate under principles that don't promote lasting success, they don't achieve it. People of excellence are not lazy; they know that paying attention to details is important.

COMPROMISE

Compromise is the enemy of success and the opposite of excellence. To be excellent means to go the extra mile and do even more than required. The late Golda Meir, a former prime minister of Israel, said, "To be or not to be is not a question of compromise. Either you be or you don't be."[22] Compromise is all around us these days. People say, "Oh, it's just a little thing. It can't possibly hurt." But little things do hurt. When we compromise, it hurts God and it hurts us. It may ultimately hurt our lives and futures. To be people of excellence and integrity we must have a set of standards we live by and refuse to change them when they are not convenient.

Compromise is the opposite of excellence.

EXCELLENCE IS A CHOICE

To be excellent is a choice. It affects all our decisions and every aspect of our lives. I say excellence is a choice because we must *decide* to be excellent. Otherwise, we may allow our fleshly nature to lead us, and the flesh is always mediocre even at its best. Mediocrity is halfway between success and failure.

Here are some simple, practical ways you can begin to practice excellence:

- Always put things back where you got them.
- Don't leave messes for other people to clean up.
- If you are given too much change or not charged for an item in a store, return the extra money or ask the clerk to charge you for the item that was overlooked.
- Always say "I'm sorry" when you hurt or offend someone.
- If your job allows a half hour for lunch, don't take thirty-five minutes, thinking the extra time doesn't matter.

- Don't take office supplies—such as pens, paper clips, notepads, and other items—home for your personal use.
- If you are in business, keep your place of business clean and organized.
- Train your employees to take pride in their workplace and keep it neat and clean.
- Practice good manners. Say "please" and "thank you."
- Be thankful and don't complain.
- If you use the last tissue in a box, put out a new box.
- If you use the last of the toilet paper, put out a new roll.
- If you drink the last cup of coffee in the coffeemaker, make a fresh pot.
- If you use all the paper in the printer or copier, refill it.

These are just a few suggestions, but you will find that the choice to be either excellent or mediocre will confront you many times each day. I believe that if you make a commitment to be excellent, it will help you in significant ways to be successful in every area of life. I can even go so far as to say that I believe it will change your life.

I have mentioned that how we treat people is very important to our success. The Bible says we should earnestly desire the greatest and best gifts, but that there is a "more excellent way," which is love (1 Corinthians 12:31 AMPC). If we focused more on showing love to people and less on getting what we want, we would be happier and more powerful. Then we could trust God to give us what He wants us to have when the time is right for us to have it. What He gives us will more than likely be better than what we wanted.

Focus more on showing love to people and less on getting what you want.

WHAT IS INTEGRITY?

If you were to ask people today what integrity is, I think many of them would probably have no idea. This is tragic. We not only need to resurrect the word *integrity* in our culture, but we also need to model it in our lives. Integrity is being honest, keeping our word, and having strong morals. It is also the state of being whole or undivided. In other words, people of integrity don't say one thing and do another. They don't live one life when people are watching and another when nobody is watching. Actually, God is always watching, and we should live with this in mind.

Those of us who have the privilege of teaching God's Word should teach principles of integrity and help people understand the importance of it. Paul told Titus to set an example by doing what is good and in his teaching to "show integrity [and] seriousness" (Titus 2:7).

Consider what these scriptures teach us about integrity:

- According to Proverbs 20:7, righteous people who walk in integrity are blessed, and so are their children (ESV).
- David writes in Psalm 101:2, "I will walk within my house in integrity and with a blameless heart" (AMPC). This means he walked

with integrity in the privacy of his home, when no one was looking.

- Psalm 15:4 says that the one who fears and honors the Lord keeps their word "even when it hurts, and does not change their mind." This means that you should tell the truth even if it causes you to have problems.

God promotes people who live with integrity.

God promotes people who live with integrity. Being a person of integrity may cost you initially, but it will pay off later. Here is a story about that.

Monty Roberts grew up around horses in California. His father was a horse trainer and Monty was riding before he learned to walk. This was during the heyday of Western Movies and as a child Monty rode horses in movies, often as a stunt double for child actors. He later got into

rodeos and horse shows and earned a reputation
as a great horseman.

Roberts always dreamed of being a horse
trainer himself, and with a wife and a couple
of kids to support he figured it was time to get
serious, so he went into the business. In spite
of his reputation as a great rider, Roberts was
an inexperienced trainer, and had trouble getting clients. He had only 4 horses to train which
wasn't bringing in nearly enough money to support his family.

Roberts wasn't sure what he was going to do
when an opportunity was presented to work
as an apprentice with Don Dodge, one of the
most well-known and well-respected trainers in
the area. He was told to bring two of his horses
with him.

After 10 weeks the apprenticeship ended and
Roberts met with Dodge. One of the horses he
had brought with him was named Panama Buck.
Dodge told Roberts that when he got home he
should call up the horse's owner, Lawson Williams, and tell him that he was wasting his money

having Roberts train the horse because the horse was never going to amount to anything.

Roberts was understandably reluctant to do this, as that would eliminate a quarter of his already meager income. When he asked Dodge why he should do this, Dodge responded that the most important thing he could do was always tell owners the truth about their horses, and if he did this he would soon get more than enough business to replace the loss.

Roberts went home and did as instructed but Williams didn't take the news well. He responded by berating Roberts, screaming, "You useless son of a gun, you wouldn't know a good horse if it leapt up between your legs. That's the last horse you'll ever get from me!"

Several days later Roberts's phone rang. A voice on the other end said, "Hello, Mr. Gray here, Joe Gray." He went on, "I was having lunch with Mr. Williams yesterday. He was complaining about you, but from what I heard you must be about the only honest trainer I ever heard of. Well, I know that Panama Buck horse of his wasn't any good, and I just want to take a flyer on you. I have this horse I want to send to you; it's called My Blue Heaven."

From that point on things started to turn around for Roberts. He gained a reputation as not only a great trainer, but an honest one, and soon he had more than enough horses to train. Eventually he would even have the opportunity to train horses for the Queen of England. And it all started with following some wise advice from a mentor to always be honest, even when the price is high.[23]

I wholeheartedly believe that following the principles of excellence and integrity is the reason God has blessed our ministry so much. I also believe that, as you follow them, your life will be blessed.

11

❧

Twelve Rules for Success

❧

*True success has more components than one
sentence or idea can contain.*

Zig Ziglar[24]

I want to remind you of twelve things I think are valuable to remember on your journey to success. Several of them are reminders of material I have already covered and several are new, but each one is important for you to succeed.

1. ALWAYS KEEP GOD FIRST.

Do everything you do with God and for God. Do it all for His glory and praise. Romans 11:36 says, "For from Him, and through Him, and to Him are all things. To Him be the glory forever. Amen" (NASB).

In addition, keep your conscience clear so nothing hinders your relationship with God. I believe the success of everything in life depends on our relationship with God.

2. HAVE A GOAL OR A DREAM THAT IS CLEAR IN YOUR HEART.

Don't be afraid to step out and try to follow the dream God has put in your heart. If you make mistakes, which we all do, learn from them. Ask the Holy Spirit to guide you as you go after your dreams, and be faithful to follow where He leads. Don't try so hard to please other people that you end up doing something you dislike simply to keep them happy.

Don't try so hard to please others that you do something you don't like just to keep them happy.

---

3. LOVE YOURSELF IN A BALANCED WAY.

Loving yourself in a balanced way does not mean being selfish. It means taking care of yourself, remembering that God created you in His image, and believing that you are not a mistake. God loves you unconditionally and wants you to have a good relationship with yourself. Learn to see yourself as God sees you. Success is impossible if you have a poor self-image.

4. STRIVE TO BE THE KIND OF PERSON GOD WANTS YOU TO BE BEFORE YOU TRY TO SUCCEED AT ANYTHING ELSE.

Remember what Jesus says in Matthew 6:33: "But seek first his kingdom and his righteousness, and all these things will be given to you as well."

Unless you become the person God wants you to be, any success you achieve will come with a sense of frustration. I'm not saying we have to be perfect. God is gracious, and He blesses us while we are on our way to becoming who He wants us to be. But people who are not on that journey tend to feel that something is missing, no matter what they achieve.

5. REMAIN PEACEFUL AT ALL TIMES.

I believe that being at peace is so important to success that I want to elaborate on it. Jesus is the Prince of Peace (Isaiah 9:6), and He gives us His peace (John 14:27). In the Amplified Bible, Classic Edition John 14:27 goes on to say, "Stop allowing yourselves to be agitated and disturbed." So Jesus gives us His peace, but to receive it, we need to stop letting ourselves get upset. Anger is all around us these days, and if we want to remain peaceful, we must understand the importance of peace and be committed to it. Don't let angry people irritate you and thereby bring you down to their level.

Where there is peace there is power. I mentioned earlier that God clearly instructed me to keep strife out of my life and ministry. I can say without hesitation that this is a full-time job. Satan knows the dangers of strife, turmoil, and anger, and he works diligently to bring division between people who are trying to work together. If you want to build anything significant, you will have to work with other people, which means there is potential for strife. I have found that the best way to keep strife out of my life is to confront it.

The best way to keep strife from your life is to confront it.

Ronald Reagan said, "Peace is not the absence of conflict, but the ability to cope with conflict by peaceful means."[25] It is impossible to live and never have conflict, but we can learn to handle conflict properly, or, as I often say, we can learn to disagree agreeably. Paul told the Corinthians that they were still unspiritual because they were jealous and their relationships involved strife with others (1 Corinthians 3:3 AMP).

Strife includes bickering, arguing, heated disagreement, and an angry undercurrent running through situations or relationships. I think the angry undercurrent is the most dangerous aspect of strife. This happens when people pretend that all is well but behind the scenes are gossiping, judging, and even hating. Strife destroys any hope of success in business, ministry, and relationships. Psalm 133 teaches that where there is unity there will be blessing. Because this is true, we would also conclude that where there is no unity, there is no blessing.

Strife destroys all hope of success in life.

Strife also offends and grieves the Holy Spirit (Ephesians 4:29–31). Because He lives in us as believers in Jesus, if He is grieved, we will also feel grieved. This kind of grief often manifests itself as depression.

Proverbs 13:10 says, "Where there is strife, there is pride." The opposite of pride is humility, so humility helps us avoid strife.

Humility is a fruit of the Holy Spirit, but it is difficult to develop. The human ego is strong, and humbling ourselves in order to avoid strife is challenging for most people. We work hard to try to look right in every situation, but as my son once said, "Being right is highly overrated." When we initiate strife with another person to prove we are right, we don't feel better because we have been found to be right. In fact, in the end, we may have damaged a relationship or lost a friend.

First Peter 3:11 teaches us to seek and pursue peace with God, with other people, and with ourselves (AMPC). I want to highlight that we must seek and pursue peace in order to have it. Satan is constantly trying to stir up trouble. He is good at this, so we should train ourselves to recognize strife at its onset and immediately do our part to stop it.

You must pursue peace in order to have it.

6. STAY FOCUSED.

Focus is difficult to maintain in our busy lives, yet it is necessary if we want to succeed at anything. If I want to study God's Word, I must be able to remain focused for the period of time I have set aside to study. If you and I attended a seminar and didn't remain focused on what was being taught, we could sit through the entire presentation and leave unable to remember anything that was said. When I write a book, I always try to go to a place where I won't be distracted. I prefer to be totally alone, because every time I get distracted, I then have to spend precious time to regain my focus.

Technology can make it challenging—but not impossible—to stay focused on anything for long. We don't have to answer the phone every time it rings or check our email every few minutes. We can even turn off the phone for a few hours. In addition to technology, Satan will use well-meaning people you love and care about to distract you. They will need you to do something or feel they cannot wait to talk to you. Even then, unless they have a true emergency, you must be assertive enough to say "No, I can't do that right now, but I'll get back to you."

Most days include many distractions, but we can find ways to minimize or avoid them. I have heard that we cannot do everything and do anything right, and I believe it. Therefore, decide what you want to accomplish each day and determine to stay focused on it.

7. BE PATIENT.

We hear people say "That person was an overnight success." This is not true. There are no overnight successes. True, lasting success in anything requires time and patience. We have much to learn on the pathway to success, and God usually matures and develops us gradually.

We sometimes see people who are put on a platform quickly because they have an outstanding gift or ability. But if they don't have the maturity to go along with their gift, they almost always end up behaving immaturely, getting themselves into trouble, and losing the opportunity they had. Paul advised Timothy not to put new believers into a place of leadership because they could become filled with pride and then fall (1 Timothy 3:6).

Fast and fragile, slow and solid.

I always wanted everything to happen fast in the ministry, but Dave was content to be patient and wait. He had a saying that frustrated me at the time, but I now know is true: "Fast and fragile, slow and solid."

Scripture teaches that we obtain God's promises through faith and patience (Hebrews 6:12). Patience is a fruit of the Holy Spirit (Galatians 5:22–23) that grows only under trial, according to *Vine's Dictionary of Greek Words*. Patience is not the ability to wait; it is staying faithful and emotionally stable *while* we wait. Waiting is not an option. We all wait for many things, but not everyone waits well. If we don't know how to wait patiently for what we desire, we make ourselves miserable. Impatience is useless because it doesn't make things happen faster.

Patience is staying faithful while you wait.

---

8. THINK AND SPEAK WHAT YOU WANT, NOT WHAT YOU HAVE.

God calls things that don't exist as though they already do (Romans 4:17). What is the point in praying for God to deliver your child from a drug addiction and then going to lunch with a friend and talking about how afraid you are that they will never be set free? It would be far better to say something like "I believe God is working in my child's life, and I will see the day when this child is completely free from drug addiction."

When you have a dream for your life, get your thoughts into agreement with your desire. When you pray, tell God you look forward to the day when you see it happen. I had to wait a long time to see the full-ness of my dreams come to pass, but I also had to learn to be thankful for what I did see, even when it was small compared to what I saw in my heart. I worked in ministry for ten years before I ever started Joyce Meyer Ministries. Those ten years were formative ones. During that important season, a foundation was laid for the future. Those years were also difficult, but that is only because I didn't understand what I understand now. The only way to get to the good times is to go through the hard times, which are almost always learning times.

Anything worth having is worth working for.

If we run from difficulty, we will spend our lives looking for something that is easy. But anything really worth having is worth working for and waiting for.

9. DEVELOP A STRONG WORK ETHIC.

"A dream comes with much business and painful effort" (Ecclesiastes 5:3 AMPC). Dave and I worked so hard in the beginning years of our ministry that I sometimes wonder how we did it. But desire motivates us like nothing else does, and God gives us the grace to do what He has called us to do.

I admit that I mistakenly said yes to some things I should not have agreed to do. But as I have said often, we learn from our mistakes. It is important not to go beyond the grace God gives us in our lives. His grace is His ability and power enabling us to do things with ease. God invites us to enter His rest, which I believe, as I mentioned in chapter 2, is a rest *while* we work, not a rest *from* work.

Do not go beyond the grace God gives you.

Balance and moderation are important to avoiding burnout. Many people wear themselves out because they don't live balanced lives. I have worked so hard at times that I made myself sick. The last time I did this, I didn't get over it quickly. Because of this, I finally learned that although we have to be ready to work hard, there comes a time when we need to let other people do many things we once did. God will give you the help you need if you will use it.

One more piece of advice along these lines is to not compare yourself with anyone else. Some people have a great capacity for work, while others need more rest. Don't try to be someone else, and don't judge others for not being like you are. Some people work quickly, while others work slowly. It took me a long time to learn this lesson. I started out thinking everyone should be like I was. All that did was frustrate me and cause me to judge them, which is an ungodly behavior.

10. BE GOOD TO PEOPLE.

No one succeeds alone. Even if you are the owner of a business or the leader of a ministry or organization, you can't do everything by yourself. It's important to have people around you who will support you, encourage you, pray for you, and even help you with practical aspects of your life. I am thankful for the people who help me in all these ways.

As I mentioned earlier, I make a priority of treating

people well. I am committed to paying our ministry employees well and offering them benefits that are valuable to them. I want them to hear compliments, to be encouraged, and to know how much we appreciate them. I want working for Joyce Meyer Ministries to be a blessing to them. I could not do what I do without the great team we have, and they all share in our success.

When people help you succeed, be as good and generous to them as you possibly can. Recognize how important they are to you. Compliment and affirm them. Pay them the best you can, and offer benefits that help them feel cared for and appreciated.

In addition, be good to people in your community, your nation, and the world who are in need. If you have the money to do so, give financially to a ministry that serves the poor. If you have more time than money, consider delivering meals to people through a food ministry, or simply go through your closet and give extra clothes and shoes to places that will make them available to people in need.

You can find lots of ways to be good and generous to people. Even a smile can make someone's day. I don't believe anyone achieves true success if they keep their resources to themselves. Real success, God's way, involves blessing and being good to other people.

11. TAKE TIME TO ENJOY YOUR LIFE.

During many of the years I worked so hard, I didn't take time to enjoy life or to even enjoy the ministry. You may remember God took time after each thing He created—He looked it over, said it was good, and approved it (Genesis 1). We need to celebrate each little bit of progress we make instead of grumbling about how far we still have to go.

According to John 10:10, the enemy comes to steal, kill, and destroy. But Jesus came that we might have life and enjoy our lives and have them "to the full" until they overflow (AMPC). Because I grew up in a dysfunctional, incestuous home, I never learned how to relax and enjoy life. I was always waiting in fear for the next episode of anger or abuse. When I was in my twenties, I could not remember ever enjoying life. I listened to Dave talk about how much fun he had as a child, even though his family had very little, and although I was happy for him, it made me realize I had no pleasant memories.

God had to teach me how to enjoy my journey. I always felt more valuable when I was working, and anytime I tried to enjoy anything, I felt guilty. God showed me that I felt guilty because I didn't think I deserved to have enjoyment. I was still punishing myself for things that were not even my fault.

I learned that no matter how much I worked, there would always be more to do, and that taking breaks to do things I enjoyed made me more creative when I went back to work. I will be forever grateful that God taught me how to live a balanced life that includes worship, work, and play. We are tripart beings (spirit, soul, and body) and we must take care of ourselves spiritually, mentally, emotionally, physically, socially, financially, and in every other way.

I urge you to take regular time off from work. Rest, enjoy your hobbies, read fiction, play golf, watch movies, or do whatever you enjoy. But I also urge you to realize that success requires seasons of hard work. Stay balanced and you won't open any doors for the devil. Remember, 1 Peter 5:8 says, "Be well balanced (temperate, sober of mind), be vigilant and cautious at all times; for that enemy of yours, the devil, roams around like a lion roaring [in fierce hunger], seeking someone to seize upon and devour" (AMPC). The devil is looking for someone to devour, but it doesn't have to be you or me if we use wisdom and follow the guidance of the Holy Spirit.

12. NEVER GIVE UP.

I'm not good at quitting! The Bible tells us not to be weary in well doing (doing right) because we will reap a harvest "in due season" if we do not give up (Galatians 6:9 KJV). Due season is not always the season we would like it to be. It is God's appointed time, and His timing is always perfect.

There are thousands of great stories about people who faced failure after failure and ended up being extremely successful because they didn't give up. For example, Elvis Presley's music teacher remarked that he "had no aptitude for music."[26] And Dr. Seuss presented his first book to more than twenty publishers before it was finally accepted—his books went on to sell more than 700 million copies.[27]

It seems obvious that if you believe you have something worthwhile to offer, you should believe in it, no matter what anyone else says. That's what I did. Now I preach in meetings attended by thousands of people. But when I started, I did hundreds of meetings attended by one hundred or fewer people. I recall one meeting with only nine people—and five of them went to the meeting with me! You might ask if this was discouraging, and the answer is yes, but not discouraging enough to make me quit. I think that when God puts something in you, the desire to do it is so strong that it pushes you forward in the face of all kinds of adversity.

Each failure is a stepping-stone. The only way you can fail is to give up. Here are some things to never give up on:

- Never give up on your health. You can be healthy and feel great.
- Never give up on those you love. God can change them.

- Never give up on your finances. You can be debt-free.
- Never give up on your dreams. You can see them become a reality.
- Never give up on yourself. You can overcome fear, shyness, lack of confidence, and anything else you need to overcome.

The devil loves quitters. Don't ever give him the satisfaction of seeing you give up. If you just keep moving forward, you will succeed.

Conclusion

Sometimes it takes us a while to find just the right fit for us, but you will find it if you keep talking with God and stepping out in faith. Sometimes you have to step back and start again, but there is a place that is right for you. Don't give up until you find it.

God has given someone the desire and ability to do every job that needs to be done. Always remember that your part is important, whether you are a ditch digger, a nanny, a preacher, a business tycoon, a banker, a window washer, a stay-at-home mom who home-schools her children, or any number of other things. Don't compare yourself with anyone else. Just be the best "you" you can be, and do it for God's glory. That's the pathway to true success.

Do you have a real relationship with Jesus?

God loves you! He created you to be a special, unique, one-of-a-kind individual, and He has a specific purpose and plan for your life. And through a personal relationship with your Creator—God—you can discover a way of life that will truly satisfy your soul.

No matter who you are, what you've done, or where you are in your life right now, God's love and grace are greater than your sin—your mistakes. Jesus willingly gave His life so you can receive forgiveness from God and have new life in Him. He's just waiting for you to invite Him to be your Savior and Lord.

If you are ready to commit your life to Jesus and follow Him, all you have to do is ask Him to forgive your sins and give you a fresh start in the life you are meant to live. Begin by praying this prayer . . .

Lord Jesus, thank You for giving Your life
for me and forgiving me of my sins so I can have
a personal relationship with You. I am sincerely
sorry for the mistakes I've made, and I know
I need You to help me live right.

Your Word says in Romans 10:9, "If you declare
with your mouth, 'Jesus is Lord,' and believe in
your heart that God raised him from the dead,
you will be saved" (NIV). I believe You are the Son
of God and confess You as my Savior and Lord.
Take me just as I am, and work in my heart,
making me the person You want me to be.
I want to live for You, Jesus, and I am so grateful
that You are giving me a fresh start in my
new life with You today.
I love You, Jesus!

It's so amazing to know that God loves us so much! He
wants to have a deep, intimate relationship with us that
grows every day as we spend time with Him in prayer and
Bible study. And we want to encourage you in your new
life in Christ.

Please visit joycemeyer.org/KnowJesus to request Joyce's
book *A New Way of Living*, which is our gift to you. We also
have other free resources online to help you make progress
in pursuing everything God has for you.

Congratulations on your fresh start in your life in Christ!
We hope to hear from you soon.

Source Notes

Unless otherwise noted, Scripture quotations are taken from the Holy Bible, New International Version®, NIV®. Copyright ©1973, 1978, 1984, 2011 by Biblica, Inc.™ Used by permission of Zondervan. All rights reserved worldwide. www.zondervan.com. The "NIV" and "New International Version" are trademarks registered in the United States Patent and Trademark Office by Biblica, Inc.™

Scripture quotations marked AMPC are taken from the Amplified® Bible. Copyright © 1954, 1958, 1962, 1964, 1965, 1987 by The Lockman Foundation. Used by permission. www.lockman.org.

Scripture quotations marked AMP are from the Amplified® Bible. Copyright © 2015 by The Lockman Foundation. Used by permission. www.lockman.org.

Scripture quotations marked NKJV are taken from the New King James Version®. Copyright © 1982 by Thomas Nelson. Used by permission. All rights reserved.

Scripture quotations marked ESV are taken from The Holy Bible, English Standard Version. ESV® Text Edition: 2016. Copyright © 2001 by Crossway Bibles, a publishing ministry of Good News Publishers.

Scripture quotations marked NASB are taken from the New American Standard Bible®, copyright © 1960, 1971, 1977, 1995, 2020 by The Lockman Foundation. All rights reserved.

Scripture quotations marked KJV are taken from the King James Version of the Bible.

1. "Albert Schweitzer Quotes," BrainyQuote, https://www.brainyquote .com/quotes/albert_schweitzer_15598.

2. "Michael R. Phillips: Quotes," Goodreads, https://www.goodreads .com/quotes/18785-the-best-things-are-never-arrived-at-in-haste-god.

3. "Albert Einstein Quotes," BrainyQuote, https://www.brainyquote.com /quotes/albert_einstein_131187.

4. "Mark Twain Quotes," Goodreads, https://www.goodreads.com /quotes/83918-the-worst-loneliness-is-to-not-be-comfortable-with -yourself.

5. Martin Luther, Letter to Melanchthon, 1521.

6. "Colin Powell Quotes," BrainyQuote, https://www.brainyquote.com /quotes/colin_powell_121363.

7. Mark Batterson, "Everything I Need to Know I Learned from the Wise Men," December 23, 2018, https://national.cc/media/let-there -be-light/everything-i-need-to-know-i-learned-from-the-wise-men -2018.

8. "Norman Vincent Peale Quotes," BrainyQuote, https://www .brainyquote.com/quotes/norman_vincent_peale_130593.

9. "Michelangelo Quotes," BrainyQuote, https://www.brainyquote .com/quotes/michelangelo_108779.

10. Kevin Daum, "21 Quotes from Thomas Jefferson That Will Inspire You," *Inc.*, April 12, 2016, https://www.inc.com/kevin-daum/21 -quotes-from-thomas-jefferson-that-will-inspire-you.html.

11. "J.C. Penney Quotes," Finest Quotes, http://www.finestquotes.com /author_quotes-author-J.C.+Penney-page-0.htm.

12. "Seneca Quotes," BrainyQuote, https://www.brainyquote.com/quotes /seneca_405078.

13. "Theodore Roosevelt Quotes," BrainyQuote, https://www
    .brainyquote.com/quotes/theodore_roosevelt_122116.

14. Steven R. Covey, *The 7 Habits of Highly Effective People 30th
    Anniversary Card Deck eBook Companion* (Mango Media, 2022).

15. David Nield, "Humans Can Really Only Maintain Five Close
    Friends, According to This Equation," Science Alert, May 3, 2016,
    https://www.sciencealert.com/the-latest-data-suggests-you-can-only
    -keep-five-close-friends.

16. Franklin Graham, Billy Graham, and Donna Lee Toney, *Billy
    Graham in Quotes* (Thomas Nelson, 2011).

17. Pass It On, https//:www.passiton.com/inspirational-quotes/6476-the
    -dictionary-is-the-only-place-that-success-comes-before-work.

18. "Margaret Thatcher Quotes," BrainyQuote, https://www
    .brainyquote.com/quotes/margaret_thatcher_114264.

19. Martin H. Manser, ed., *The Westminster Collection of Christian
    Quotations* (Westminster John Knox Press, 2001), 76.

20. "Plato Quotes," BrainyQuote, https://brainyquote.com/quotes/plato
    _108514.

21. AZ Quotes, https://azquotes.com/quote/584747.

22. Israel Shenker, "Mrs. Meir, at Princeton, Offers Her Views," *New York
    Times*, December 12, 1974, https://www.nytimes.com/1974/12/12
    /archives/mrs-meir-at-princeton-offers-her-views-her-constituency.html.

23. "A Story of Integrity," Soares Martial Arts, February 19, 2020,
    https://lsfmac.com/a-story-of-integrity.

24. Zig Ziglar and Tom Ziglar, *Born to Win: Find Your Success Code*
    (Ziglar Success Books, 2012).

25. Ronald Reagan, "Commencement Address, Eureka College," May 9,
    1982, https://www.reaganfoundation.org/ronald-reagan/reagan
    -quotes-speeches/commencement-address-eureka-college.

26. Orsolya Plesz, "Elvis Presley—a Biography," *Manchester Historian*,
    June 6, 2017, https://manchesterhistorian.com/2017/elvis-presley
    -a-biography.

27. Danny McLoughlin, "Dr. Seuss Statistics," WordsRated, November
    2, 2022, https://wordsrated.com/dr-seuss-statistics.

About the Author

Joyce Meyer is one of the world's leading practical Bible teachers and a *New York Times*–bestselling author. Joyce's books have helped millions of people find hope and restoration through Jesus Christ. Joyce's program, *Enjoying Everyday Life*, is broadcast on television, radio, and online to millions worldwide in over one hundred languages.

Through Joyce Meyer Ministries, Joyce teaches internationally on a number of topics with a particular focus on how the Word of God applies to our everyday lives. Her candid communication style allows her to share openly and practically about her experiences so others can apply what she has learned to their lives.

Joyce has authored more than 140 books, which have been translated into more than 160 languages, and over 39 million of her books have been distributed worldwide. Bestsellers include *Power Thoughts*; *The Confident Woman*; *Look Great, Feel Great*; *Starting Your Day Right*; *Ending Your Day Right*; *Approval Addiction*;

How to Hear from God; *Beauty for Ashes*; and *Battlefield of the Mind*.

Joyce's passion to help people who are hurting is foundational to the vision of Hand of Hope, the missions arm of Joyce Meyer Ministries. Each year Hand of Hope provides millions of meals for the hungry and malnourished, installs freshwater wells in poor and remote areas, provides critical relief after natural disasters, and offers free medical and dental care to thousands through their hospitals and clinics worldwide. Through Project GRL, women and children are rescued from human trafficking and provided safe places to receive an education, nutritious meals, and the love of God.

JOYCE MEYER MINISTRIES
U.S. & FOREIGN OFFICE ADDRESSES

Joyce Meyer Ministries
P.O. Box 655
Fenton, MO 63026
USA
(636) 349-0303

Joyce Meyer Ministries—Canada
P.O. Box 7700
Vancouver, BC V6B 4E2
Canada
(800) 868-1002

Joyce Meyer Ministries—Australia
Locked Bag 77
Mansfield Delivery Centre
Queensland 4122
Australia
(07) 3349 1200

Joyce Meyer Ministries—England
P.O. Box 1549
Windsor SL4 1GT
United Kingdom
01753 831102

Joyce Meyer Ministries—South Africa
P.O. Box 5
Cape Town 8000
South Africa
(27) 21-701-1056

Joyce Meyer Ministries—Francophonie
29 avenue Maurice Chevalier
77330 Ozoir la Ferriere
France

Joyce Meyer Ministries—Germany
Postfach 761001
22060 Hamburg
Germany
+49 (0)40 / 88 88 4 11 11

Joyce Meyer Ministries—Netherlands
Lorenzlaan 14
7002 HB Doetinchem
+31 657 555 9789

Joyce Meyer Ministries—Russia
P.O. Box 789
Moscow 101000
Russia
+7 (495) 727-14-68

Other Books by Joyce Meyer

100 Inspirational Quotes

100 Ways to Simplify Your Life

21 Ways to Finding Peace and Happiness

The Answer to Anxiety

Any Minute

Approval Addiction

The Approval Fix

Authentically, Uniquely You*

The Battle Belongs to the Lord

Battlefield of the Mind*

Battlefield of the Mind Bible

Battlefield of the Mind for Kids

Battlefield of the Mind for Teens

Battlefield of the Mind Devotional

Battlefield of the Mind New Testament

Be Anxious for Nothing*

Being the Person God Made You to Be

Beauty for Ashes

Change Your Words, Change Your Life

Colossians: A Biblical Study

The Confident Mom

The Confident Woman

The Confident Woman Devotional

Joyce Meyer Spanish Titles

Auténtica y única
(Authentically, Uniquely You)

Belleza en lugar de cenizas
(Beauty for Ashes)

Buena salud, buena vida
(Good Health, Good Life)

Cambia tus palabras, cambia tu vida
(Change Your Words, Change Your Life)

El campo de batalla de la mente
(Battlefield of the Mind)

Cómo envejecer sin avejentarse
(How to Age without Getting Old)

Como formar buenos habitos y romper malos habitos
(Making Good Habits, Breaking Bad Habits)

La conexión de la mente
(The Mind Connection)

Dios no está enojado contigo
(God Is Not Mad at You)

La dosis de aprobación
(The Approval Fix)

Efesios: Comentario biblico
(Ephesians: Biblical Commentary)

Empezando tu día bien
(Starting Your Day Right)

Hágalo con miedo
(Do It Afraid)

Hazte un favor a ti mismo…perdona
(Do Yourself a Favor…Forgive)

Madre segura de sí misma
(The Confident Mom)

Momentos de quietud con Dios
(Quiet Times with God Devotional)

Mujer segura de sí misma
(The Confident Woman)

No se afane por nada
(Be Anxious for Nothing)

Pensamientos de poder
(Power Thoughts)

Sanidad para el alma de una mujer
(Healing the Soul of a Woman)

Sanidad para el alma de una mujer, devocionario
(Healing the Soul of a Woman Devotional)

Santiago: Comentario bíblico
(James: Biblical Commentary)

Sobrecarga
(Overload)*

Sus batallas son del Señor
(Your Battles Belong to the Lord)

Termina bien tu día
(Ending Your Day Right)

Tienes que atreverte
(I Dare You)

Usted puede comenzar de nuevo
(You Can Begin Again)

Viva amando su vida
(Living a Life You Love)

Viva valientemente
(Living Courageously)

Vive por encima de tus sentimientos
(Living beyond Your Feelings)

* Study Guide available for this title

Books by Dave Meyer

Life Lines